THE COLLEGE FROM WITHIN

The College from Within

MONROE E. DEUTSCH
VICE-PRESIDENT AND PROVOST, EMERITUS
UNIVERSITY OF CALIFORNIA

1952

UNIVERSITY OF CALIFORNIA PRESS
BERKELEY AND LOS ANGELES

University of California Press · Berkeley and Los Angeles, California
Cambridge University Press · London · England
Copyright 1952
By the Regents of the University of California
Printed in the United States of America
By the University of California Press
Designed by Ward Ritchie

Second Printing

TO A.F.D.

Preface

WHEN an officer in the Army has completed his campaigns and ended his service, he is tempted to write an account of war as he saw it and record the conclusions he has drawn from his career. Similarly a government official, when his term is ended, is likely to tell his story and indicate wherein, from his point of view, wise steps were taken or mistakes were made. May not, therefore, the retired professor be forgiven if he either depicts his own career as he sees it in review, as Bliss Perry and John Erskine have done, or at least discusses some of the features of higher education in the United States as he has seen them—features constituting its strength and its weakness? At any rate here is one university official, or rather a onetime official, who feels impelled to do the latter.

Let me emphasize that these are personal judgments, personal views. While inevitably in the course of his life the author has read articles and books touching on these problems, and above all has discussed them in committee meetings and over the luncheon table at the Faculty Club, it should be reiterated that the conclusions reached are wholly his own and that no attempt whatsoever has been made to read the numerous books and countless articles which treat of the modern college and university. Indeed, if that attempt had been made, I feel sure the book would never have been written, since by no possibility would there have been time enough to plow through the mass of material that has appeared in print.

And, after all, the opinions that have developed in the mind of one man after long years of experience may not be uninteresting and possibly may even be useful to others engaged in college work, and indeed to those members of the general public who realize the important part that higher education plays or should play in our national life.

I might say, "Any resemblance to practices in existing institutions is purely coincidental," but I cannot. However, what is here outlined is a composite of procedures in various colleges; at times proposals are advanced that, as far as is known to me, are not in operation anywhere. The views are derived from personal experience, modified and shaped by conferences with colleagues in various institutions.

The purpose of the book is to set forth frankly and honestly conclusions that have gradually developed and crystallized, with the hope that thereby thought on those problems may be stimulated and occasionally even action may result.

I am grateful to the various publishers who have permitted me to use quotations from the books or periodicals which they have issued; in each case due credit is given.

And I must express my thanks to those who have assisted me in many different ways; they have, of course, no responsibility for the opinions expressed. My appreciation goes to Professors George R. Stewart, Benjamin H. Lehman, and Paul B. Schaeffer, Miss Carolyn Anspacher, Mr. George Lichty, Mr. Donald Coney, Miss Eugenie Carneiro, Mr. Frank E. Robbins, *and Dean David Snodgrass. The help of Mr. Harold A. Small and Professor Emeritus William H. Alexander, of the University of California Press, has been invaluable; Mr. August Frugé, Manager of the Publishing Department, has carefully supervised the details of publication. To all of these I am greatly indebted.*

M. E. D.

Contents

Contents

ILLUSTRATIONS
(Following page 126)

The Rotunda, University of Virginia
A REMINDER THAT THOMAS JEFFERSON SHAPED A UNIVER-
SITY BOTH ARCHITECTURALLY AND EDUCATIONALLY

Commencement at Stanford
IN THE FROST AMPHITHEATER, WITH THE HOOVER WAR
LIBRARY IN THE BACKGROUND

The Chapel at Princeton
THE LARGEST COLLEGE CHAPEL IN THE UNITED STATES,
DESIGNED BY RALPH ADAMS CRAM

Illustrations

The Library at Bryn Mawr

Wellesley: Science Laboratory, 1886

Students from Seventeen Countries, at International House, University of California, Berkeley

Candidates for Honorary Degrees, Columbia, 1947

Members of the "Sixty-five Club," Hastings College of the Law, San Francisco

Illustrations

THE COLLEGE FROM WITHIN

I.

Alma Mater

> *When youth and I lived in't together.*
> COLERIDGE, *Youth and Age*

STUDENTS, to be sure, vary greatly in what they gain intellectually from college or university. Some go forth well equipped to deal with life's problems; some are splendidly trained in the varied professions in which the university offers instruction; and some accomplish neither. But in any event, most of them, the vast majority, leave the college with a warm affection for it and its life. This is a compound of diverse elements.

There is, of course, the fact that one's students days were the days of youth; and ever afterward, college life and the life of youth with all its ideals, its romance, its yearnings, are associated in one's memory. It is the time of ambition, even more thrilling than the realization of one's hopes. It is the period of friendship; and many of those friendships become the closest of bonds throughout life. High school ties are adolescent; the associations of later years are often tinged with selfish motives and aims; but college friendships, made when maturity has come, yet free from any ulterior motives, are ties that often last for the remainder of one's days.

During those years life is fresh and exhilarating; later it may lose both qualities, but with those days

1

they will ever be identified. There is, too, a certain irresponsibility; the student is not yet the practicing physician, or lawyer, or professor. If he engages in some peccadilloes, he can do it without feeling that his status in his profession suffers.

And there is always the personal side. Among the professors there are usually some who have taken a personal interest in the student, or who have had a special appeal. Their figures form part of the background of that joyous period. Some of their idiosyncracies, their oft-repeated jokes, their mannerisms, are always good for a laugh whenever the graduates get together in reunions.

Then there are the ties of fraternity, sorority, dormitory, club; their memories are of the happy, the gay, the jovial incidents of those four years. Student activities with their hectic ambitions, their political wire-pulling, their appeals to student initiative, sometimes even their difficulties with the faculty and administration—all fit like the stones of mosaics into the picture of college days. Rallies, with the outpouring of the whole student body, bonfires blazing, speeches of coaches and of members of the team, youth at its most uninhibited; no memory of college is without these. And, above all, looms high the football season and the Big Game. Enthusiasm is unconfined, emotions are at their highest. Card stunts, the rival bands, the throngs filling the city to overflowing, cars forced to park miles from the stadium, alumni pouring back to the campus, translating all their affection for the college into the game down there on the gridiron; tenseness of the whole throng as the ball moves forward or back, joy unrestrained when a pass is successfully completed or a back gets away with the ball for a run of twenty, thirty, or more yards—the thrills of Big Game day are not only things of the moment, but form part of the memories identified with college days.

And then there is the campus itself—its buildings beautiful in memory if not always in reality, its lawns, the inscriptions on its halls, the streams that flow lazily through the grounds, the ivy covering the oldest of the buildings, the tower with its chimes. And when one walks about the grounds in the light of the full moon, nothing seems fairer, nothing is more full of romance; the bridges, the monuments, the halls, the library—all are suffused with a transfiguring light.

Senior week—graduation week—filled with festivities, freed from all scholastic responsibilities; picnic and dance and pilgrimage for the last time as students, about the familiar grounds, saying farewell to each well-known spot, and then the formal ball prolonged till the following dawn. And finally Commencement: parents present, friends assembled; procession of faculty and graduates in cap and gown; the program but a haze until the moment when the degrees are conferred and the diplomas awarded. And then the farewells, the good-byes, the last glimpse of the campus as students. Yes, it is full of memories, tugging at the heartstrings.

It is not merely romance, not merely affection, that is inspired by these college days. From them springs a loyalty to the college which sometimes expresses itself, to be sure, in rather absurd sophomoric manifestations, at others in noble and generous ways. But the college is indeed the source of love and loyalty, one of the finest loyalties of which man is capable. And thus the undergraduate sees his various extracurricular activities as a means of serving his alma mater, demonstrating his love for her. And each of the public occasions, football game, pilgrimage, or commencement, comes to a close with the "Alma Mater" song, whose words may be banal and trite, but whose air moves its sons and daughters even as the "Star-Spangled Banner" or the "Marseillaise" arouses patriotic emotions, inadequate or inappropriate though the words may be. However small or large the college, "there are those who love it," as Daniel Webster said of Dartmouth. And it is all this that, crowded into the casket of memory, abides with the collegians even after their hair is gray and the days of their activity are done. It is the priceless picture of youth that remains; to the alumnus, more precious than the diploma now lying dust-covered in the attic.

In the hearts of alumni there is a real affection for the institution; they wish their children to attend it, they love to walk the familiar paths about the campus, they are happy to get together with their friends of college days to recall the gay and amusing incidents of those four delightful years. They love her romantically, not as the pedagogue with grim face, not as the tutor of many an area of learning, but as one recalls the love of one's youth. They see her through a golden glow of sweet memories, everything unpleasant forgotten or transmuted into a jest and only the thrilling and the lovely recalled.

But heartwarming as it all is, one must remember that this is not a substitute for the education which is the aim and purpose of the college. It is a combination of many delightful elements, and lures many to college

4

halls; but does it not serve as a false substitute for the things for which the university exists? The football game has nothing to do with *Veritas,* nor have the bonfires blazing at the rallies any relation to *Let There Be Light.* Yet, as some students in every college know, it is possible for the two to live together. A college can be a site of learning and education and, at the same time, warm the heart with affection. Here too, as in so many other aspects of life, it is the false emphasis that must be eradicated. We should love Alma Mater all the more if she were not merely the romantic attendant of youth, but, as her name indicates, the nourishing mother, training her sons and daughters to a richer life.

II.
The President

There's such divinity doth hedge a king.

Hamlet

Pʀᴇx is the name by which the university president is usually spoken of among students and alumni, often affectionately "prexy." The resemblance to *rex* is not wholly accidental, for the president is the real source of university policy, whatever theoretically may be the position and power of the trustees and the faculty. It is he who decides whether to approve the proposal that a new school or department be established. He determines whether he will accept recommendations for promotion within the faculty and whether a certain proposed nominee shall be called to join the staff of the institution. He decides which members of the staff shall receive increases of salary and how large these shall be. To be sure, legally all these acts must be approved by the trustees and are not in effect until so approved. But wise trustees recognize their incompetence to deal with such matters. Though I fear that occasionally we find trustees who do seek to pass upon them, certainly this is not so in the better institutions of the land.

The president has, of course, numerous advisers in the form of departmental chairmen, special committees, budget committees, and deans. He may delegate authority, but the delegation itself indicates where the authority really lies. Whatever the recommendations that may be submitted to him, his is the final decision; he has to determine whether Chemistry or Home Economics shall be expanded, whether more money shall go into the upkeep of the grounds, the employment of gardeners or janitors, the repair of buildings, funds for research, new equipment or—by no means least important in these days of rising costs—increases in salary. Shall there be new appointments? What promotions shall be made? These are but illustrations of the types of questions which the president must answer. And it is in making these choices that he is the most potent force in shaping the character of the institution. If it becomes or remains a great home of scholarship, his should be a very large share of the credit, since it was he, ultimately, who decided to which activities the greatest amount of support should be given.

This at once suggests one of the important qualifications for a president—judgment of men. It is upon this that the success of executives in any field largely depends. If the president chooses his chief advisers wisely, he may lean heavily on their counsel. If his choice is poor, he will be led to make unwise decisions. Moreover, in the latter case his faculty will inevitably become dissatisfied and hostile to him.

May I be a bit personal? When I was invited to become Vice-President of the University of California, I said to President Sproul: "I shall always be frank with you and never hesitate to say that I disagree with your views, when I do." The danger a president has is the same as that of a king; the men supposed to advise and assist him will tend to become "Yes, yes" men, seeking to please the president by agreeing with him. President Sproul heartily concurred with me in this. I still feel the high importance of complete frankness on the part of a president's advisers. In an institution with which I am familiar, the president, on election to that office, chose as his chief adviser a man who clearly did not command the confidence of the faculty. I doubt if the president made any real effort to find out what the faculty thought. One of its members described this chief adviser as "smooth as a billiard ball." The lack of success of the administration was probably in large part due to this unwise choice.

Some years ago one of our very good colleges was seeking a president. A list of the qualifications he should possess was drawn up. They were to be of the following order: he was to be a great scholar, a great executive, a great public speaker, a success in securing funds, popular with alumni, faculty, and students, and a good "mixer" in the outer world. Long as this list is, it omitted what is undoubtedly a still greater qualification, namely, judgment of men. Of course, each of the items named is desirable, but I fear no institution in the country possesses or (may I say?) ever has possessed as president the supernatural being such a list presupposes. And trustees in choosing a president will have to determine which of these desiderata is in their eyes most important or (to put it in somewhat different terms) what type of institution they wish their college to become.

In my judgment the most important attribute to be sought in a president is educational leadership. As has been pointed out, his every act affects the character of the institution, and he cannot see what the effect of his decisions will inevitably be unless he has a conception of the true function of the college and lets this, like a compass, guide him in all he does. To be sure, he should constantly consult his faculty through its appropriate committees; and he will find that they will rejoice to have at the helm one who is genuinely concerned with educational problems and faces them with high ideals for his institution.

I am firmly convinced that the choice of presidents should be made from among those whose lives and thoughts have been devoted to work in colleges or universities. The businessman, the physician, the public official, and the general have none of them spent their lives in dealing with such questions; indeed, they may be tempted to let the standards of the outer world (shall I say "the market place"?) dominate their acts. A university may be large or small; nonetheless it is an educational institution, not a business. Of course, it has its business aspect, but it would be a sorry day for higher education if in our colleges the business side were to be given priority over education. The larger the institution, the greater the danger that its sheer administrative mechanism may be regarded as of the first importance. That way lies the road to academic and intellectual decline. Business must minister to the needs of education, not master it.

Not only do we find presidents chosen for administrative or business ability, but in many other ways do we see business assuming an abnormal place in the life of a university. Business officers often represent the institution at the state legislature; while they may be able glibly to furnish statistics on enrollment and so on, they are not likely to have any comprehension of what the institution really signifies or what its functions are. To be sure, such an official can become intimate with legislators as a professor never could, but the business officer will naturally be more concerned with winning than with the expense of the sacrifices that may have to be made in order to win. If a legislator makes a remark about "long-hairs" in the faculty, or even "reds," there is danger that the business official may let it go with a smile rather than defend the scholar. Far better for the president himself to make such appearances as may be necessary, than to employ a permanent lobbyist even as the liquor interests do, or the horse-racing or other lobbies. We should beware of placing too much power in the business office of an institution; its standards are often not those of the academic side of the college, and it may seek to influence the institution in the direction of sacrificing its standards for the sake of a possible financial gain or an assumed improvement in public relations. Certainly, it is rarely that I have met a business officer who did not feel the high importance of athletics, for instance, in public relations.

The university with its hard-won and indispensable rights of academic freedom—in research, in teaching, in public utterances, whether by tongue or pen—properly fears for these if a president be brought in from other fields where they do not exist or may perhaps not even be understood.

As higher education is bringing more and yet more students to the colleges of the country, the need of wise guidance and sound educational leadership on the part of its presidents becomes all the greater. If one lists the greatest of all our past university presidents, he will find that they were scholars—and indeed scholars of distinction.

It may be proposed (as I have often heard suggested) that a president who is not a scholar should delegate to his chief assistant, presumably a vice-president, all purely academic decisions. If the president actually accepts this procedure, the vice-president becomes the head so far as the real work of the university is concerned. The president is then the "front." Yet at any moment the president may overrule his associate, and will often be tempted to, and then we have the evil effects of a nonacademic decision. Moreover, is it not a topsy-turvy situation when the nominal head of an educational institution has nothing to do with its educational policies, nothing to do with any of the purposes for which it exists?

Notable examples of nonacademic appointments are, of course, General Eisenhower and Governor Stassen. The former, after his command of the allied forces in the Normandy invasion, was placed upon the inactive list of the Army. The latter, having failed to secure the Republican nomination for the Presidency in 1948, was available for some kind of appointment. Indeed, some of the backers of these men as university presidents may have had an eye upon the 1952 Presidential nomination and the importance of keeping their candidates in the limelight during the interim.

The college presidency is in danger of becoming the normal refuge of persons of prominence who are "out of a job." Indeed, Senator Robert A. Taft proposed that substantial pensions be set up for retiring Presidents of the United States so that they could afford to "accept dignified but often low-paying jobs such as college presidencies."[1] Apparently it is felt that it is the kind of position that anyone, regardless of his background, can fill.

The president, as the assumed chief of the college, will be called on to make speeches on educational topics. To be sure, he can have them "ghost-written" and utter the ideas thus concocted for his use, but it must be remembered that the ghost-writer may have views on college matters that do not represent the highest ideals of the institution. Moreover, how can a man with any self-respect talk on subjects of which he knows nothing and yet expect to carry with him the weight of authority residing in the post of president of a university?

It is urged that the president should be a capable administrator. Assuredly this is valuable, but it should never be regarded as more important than educational leadership. Yet I believe that with our host of institutions of higher learning it should not be difficult to find for a college presidency an administrative officer, as for example the president of a smaller institution or a dean, who has had administrative responsibilities and been tested in them and at the same time has never subordinated educational aims to the mechanics of administration. In every faculty, too, there are men who are regarded by their colleagues as leaders and have taken a prominent part in college affairs and served again and again on important committees of the institution. A wise president can readily find capable assistants to bear the burdens of the many details of

[1] *Time,* October 18, 1948, p. 28. Quoted by courtesy of *Time;* copyright Time Inc., 1948.

university business. Far better this solution than the selection of a man solely or primarily on the basis of administrative ability. Men selected as presidents from without the academic world are usually said to be chosen on the basis of such ability, though most of us know that fame or at least prominence of some kind plays a far greater part.

It has been pointed out that of the present-day college and university presidents some have come from nonacademic fields. This is doubtless true, particularly at minor institutions. Of the great universities it cannot often be said. The following list will make this clear: Harvard (chemistry), Princeton (political science), Chicago (philosophy), Yale (history), Michigan (zoölogy), Illinois (psychology), Minnesota (education), Ohio State (law and government), Johns Hopkins (biophysics), and Wisconsin (bacteriology). The most notable recent exceptions are Columbia and Pennsylvania.

In 1921 when the headship of the University of Pennsylvania was vacant, the trustees elected General Leonard Wood, then described as "a well-known officer and an attractive personality, after a career of distinction in the Army and in administration, now retired and available for some civil appointment."[2] He had been nominated by an alumni committee as "a man who would command universal respect, a national figure whose selection would be a financial strength, and a great administrator who can bring the University safely through its present crisis." However, General Wood asked for "successive leaves of absence

[2] Edward P. Cheyney, *History of the University of Pennsylvania, 1740–1940* (University of Pennsylvania Press, 1940), pp. 388–390.

while he accepted and continued to serve in the high office of Governor-General of the Philippines.... There were also the University Faculties who were filled with consternation at the prospect of a chief executive necessarily ignorant of the educational problems of the University, and fearful of greater emphasis on military training. The Faculty petitioned the Trustees to accept the anticipated resignation of General Wood; they declared that the head of the institution should be a man versed in education, familiar with the problems of the University, of broad views and vigorous initiative." Finally, General Wood resigned in December, 1922.

Like the greater universities, most of the better colleges have chosen presidents from academic fields.[3] It will be seen, therefore, that past experience has led trustees in general to follow the well-tried path of selecting persons with educational backgrounds, rather than "outsiders," to serve as leaders of our colleges and universities.

But the trend toward the appointment of noneducators as presidents seems to be growing greater. North Carolina recently nominated to follow President Frank P. Graham, a historian and a man of national repute, Gordon Gray, an alumnus, to be sure, and fresh from his post as Secretary of the Army; whatever his ability as a lawyer and otherwise, there is no evidence that he ever taught, or was connected with an educational institution save as a student.

---

[3] E.g., Smith (government), Swarthmore (philosophy), Vassar (political science), Mount Holyoke (English), Bryn Mawr (psychology), Amherst (economics and history), Williams (history), Bowdoin (Latin), Carleton (geology), Mills (history), and Pomona (history).

14

The President

Louisiana State University had had several unsatisfactory administrations when, four years ago, following a long and careful study by a faculty committee which unanimously recommended his appointment, Harold W. Stoke, who had been president of the University of New Hampshire, was chosen by the supervisors (as the regents of the university are called). In December, 1950, as a result of various antagonisms, springing partly from his ideal of a true university, partly from interference by the supervisors in its internal affairs, partly through his endeavor to keep athletics in their proper place, President Stoke resigned. Immediately, without consultation of the faculty by the supervisors, Lieutenant General Troy H. Middleton was chosen as his successor. What was General Middleton's career? That of an Army officer with a distinguished war record all his life, save for the period between 1937 and 1939 when he served as Dean of Administration at Louisiana State, and, after another interval of military service, his incumbency of the post of comptroller of the university from 1945 till the time when he was to become president. President Stoke, in his concluding statement, said: "Either you have a university which is devoted to the purposes a university is created to serve or you don't really have a university at all." And in reference to the procedure taken by the supervisors the faculty adopted a resolution as follows: "It is a matter of regret and concern that this body was precluded from participating in the choice of Dr. Stoke's successor."[4]

[4] The account given in this paragraph is based partly on "The Baton Rouge Story," a broadcast over station WJBO, December 29, 1950, prepared by Margaret Dixon.

The failure to recognize that a college is an educational institution, not primarily a business or an administrative organization, has just placed at the head of William and Mary College Rear Admiral Alvin Duke Chandler. Here, too, the appointment was made in haste, and the faculty had no opportunity to express itself on suitable candidates. On learning of the appointment the faculty termed it a "violation of accepted academic practice and the traditions of the college."

All these incidents tend to show that the regents or trustees may not really understand what the work of a university is. Since their official contact with the president serves to emphasize purely administrative functions, often financial, they have no conception of the fact that the president determines what kind of institution it is to be, where its emphasis shall lie, what the nature of its faculty shall be. Is this new school to be established or not? Shall this department be expanded?

The president is or should be the pilot of the ship; he doesn't merely add figures or set up a chart of administration. And this means that, on the other hand, he should not be simply a scholar absorbed in his own particular field; he must be concerned with the institution as a whole and see it as a whole. But his own scholarship makes him appreciative of scholarship in general and imbues him with a realization of its importance.

The nonacademic president is likely to be too much swayed by the external as opposed to the internal. Public relations will seem extremely important; he will be likely to be swept along by the outside current.

The outsider does not know what university ideals are, what academic freedom means or implies. To be sure, he may in general terms express himself in favor of it, even as Coolidge's clergyman declared himself against sin, but his test comes in specific acts, often remote from public view. He may be tempted to yield to outside pressure and openly or covertly seek to prevent members of the faculty from saying or writing what may offend large numbers of people or those possessed of wealth. Popularity or additional funds may well seem to him far more important than freedom to seek the truth and to express one's honest opinions. The acceptance of funds for an endowed chair under the condition that the donor is allowed to choose the incumbent is an act the impropriety of which may not even occur to the nonacademician, and the granting of an honorary degree in the hope or expectation of a financial return might seem natural to one who has been in the habit of thinking in terms of bargaining. Besides, such a president will associate far more often and more intimately with the trustees and prominent members of the community than with his faculty, and his own predisposition will thereby be strengthened.

Moreover, a nonacademic president will be particularly tempted to neglect his university duties for those activities to which he has previously devoted his life. This may involve political campaigning or even a prolonged leave of absence to accept governmental appointment or the like. On behalf of any college whose head may be offered a full-time post in the government and who desires to protect himself by requesting an extended leave of absence (perhaps even four years), I should like to point out that a leave of long duration

17

on the part of that head will unquestionably prove detrimental to the entire institution. The hands of an acting president will necessarily be tied by the very fact that he is merely an acting official. Let the president make his choice and not ask the college to incur so great a sacrifice for the sake of protecting his own security.

Hard as it is to keep one's eyes fixed on the primary aims of a college, this is made infinitely harder by the demands that come to the unfortunate president, demands that take him away from his real task. Speechmaking is one of the crosses laid upon every president. His position is assumed not only to make him an authority on education (yes, in all stages from the kindergarten through the graduate school, not excluding adult education), but on all other subjects as well. Of course, he can talk wisely (but not too wisely) and wittily on athletics before the student body and the alumni. International topics, it is assumed, are wholly within his ken. Agriculture undoubtedly he is expected to discuss, and in no amateurish manner. The service clubs regard him as fair prey; so do the parent-teacher associations, the League of Women Voters, the Association of University Women, the chambers of commerce, and teachers' institutes. Indeed, he could make, as a minimum, one speech a day if he were willing to do so. Some presidents are clever at adapting an address delivered before an organization of one type so that it can be used at a meeting of a very different nature. But if a president declines too often, he stirs up enmity and is regarded as "high-hatting" the organization which has invited him in vain. The request to speak comes frequently through a personal friend or a man or a woman of importance in the community; this makes it very difficult to refuse. And no topic is too erudite or too commonplace to be regarded as outside the knowledge of the president. Poor president!

Apposite are certain words uttered at the inauguration of one president: "Probably, Mr. President, one of your hardest tasks will be to assume the role of omniscience. You will be regarded by virtue of your presidency as an expert in all fields of human knowledge, as competent to speak on any theme proposed. Whether it be physics or philosophy, war or woman, books or banking, fisheries or football, you will be called upon to discourse on all these topics—and many more—to those who will avidly drink in your words. ... And if you state that you are not competent to treat of the subject in which the particular audience is interested, they will not believe you but will merely ascribe it to excess of modesty."[5]

Then, too, he is asked to become a director or an official of a myriad of organizations which seek the prestige his position would give. If he accepts and attends but few of the board meetings, he is the object of criticism from his fellow directors. But if he is absent from a particular meeting, he may find that action was taken at that time on some important matter in a manner to which he is entirely opposed and which may even greatly embarrass him.

And yet it is a fact that a president becomes well known primarily through his public pronouncements, be they on education, national affairs, or other topics, be they by speech, article, or book; he also becomes

---

[5] Monroe E. Deutsch, *The Letter and the Spirit* (University of California Press, 1943), p. 287.

well known by his service on various public bodies. He can only attain a national reputation by writings or addresses in numerous parts of the country. People know him by these things, not by his educational leadership within the institution or by his meticulous care in attending to the many matters that come to his desk. So there is always the greatest temptation to neglect his main task for those activities which command public attention. And it is on the basis of the latter that the public acclaims him as "a distinguished educator" and reckons him among the leading presidents of the land. The lure of such recognition, men holding the presidency often—very often—find difficult to resist. Their real task suffers as much from extracurricular activities as does the work of students.

All this involves frequent travel hither and yon. The glory of being on a committee appointed by the governor of a state or the President of the United States may lead him to accept, and the newspapers play up such membership. He flits from one meeting to another, from one town to another. And the result? Papers pile up on his desk, important decisions tend to be delayed, faculty members cannot get to see him. He loses touch with his own institution and neglects its business. The bright light of publicity and public acclaim attract the president like a moth, and his pressing duties are set aside. This is well known on the campus, but the populace judging by public appearances acclaims him a great executive. And on the basis of his position more and more external assignments are heaped upon him, leading him further and further away from the work which he was chosen to do and through which alone these pseudo-honors come to him.

The President

The president should first of all be the head of the institution, and no outside calls should be heeded which cause him to neglect that duty. Trustees should not judge him by his external activities, but should be in such close touch with the college that they are thoroughly aware whether these acts are leading to neglect of the presidential duties.

Of course, he must attend faculty meetings, faculty parties, trustees' meetings, trustees' committee meetings, athletic events, debates, important student assemblies, alumni meetings, and Heaven alone knows what else. His calendar is crowded to the full, quite aside from his necessary conferences with members of the faculty, administrative officers, student-body officers; and—not least—distinguished visitors often take it for granted they will be welcome even without an appointment.

And then there is the formal entertaining at reception, lunch, or dinner, be the visitor the governor of the state, the president of a sister university, or the ambassador from a foreign land. All these merely give a hint of the throng to whom the president is expected to extend courtesies.

Besides, he must travel. He is expected to attend national educational gatherings, to interview persons for the most important appointments to the faculty, and to address alumni gatherings far and near. There are, of course, university ceremonies, notably commencement, at which he must preside and make formal addresses. Many of the occasions mentioned involve partaking of what are euphemistically termed "banquets." He must have a hardy stomach or learn some tactful way of eating lightly or not at all.

To be sure, all institutions can well use more money than they have; it is certainly an asset if the president has the ability to indicate delicately to a possible donor the great importance of endowing a particular chair or erecting a much-needed building (to which the donor's name would, of course, be attached). But if he isn't a person possessing that particular skill, he should be able to find on his staff or add to it someone with the necessary qualifications.

Popularity with students and alumni is useful, but it should rest upon solid worth and achievements; he should not lower himself or the office which he holds by seeking through vulgar devices to secure it. He should not imitate typical politicians in order to attain popularity. The dignity which the office deserves should be respected; the attitude of the president should be neither haughty nor arrogant, but the natural expression of a fine spirit. He should be a consistent human being, living the kind of life that on serious academic occasions he urges upon his audience.

It has been pointed out that he should possess a large number of admirable traits. He should be tolerant in his dealings with others, not puritanical or austere. He should be friendly in manner. He should be coöperative in his relations with his faculty. He should be sympathetic with their problems individually and collectively. He should be persuasive in the presentation of his plans and programs. One could add a host of other highly desirable qualities. He should be genuinely intellectual and a man of broad interests. He should, in the best sense of the term, be a spiritual man; this does not necessarily mean religious in the conventional sense.

But once more we are portraying such a being as cannot be found on land or sea. Certainly, he should possess as many of these qualities as possible. But, to repeat, first and foremost still stands educational leadership, which can only come from one who is himself imbued with the spirit of the university world through having devoted his life to it as a teacher and academic officer. And to this I should join "judgment of men." Many other traits or qualities are valuable, but none can replace these two, I am convinced.

This has been admirably expressed by David Starr Jordan, the longtime president of Stanford University: "He [i.e., the president of a university] must set its pace, must frame its ideals and choose the men in whom those ideals can be realized. It is through the men he chooses that the university becomes a living person. . . . It is what he can discern and divine in other men that gauges success. It is his instinct to know what the best work of others may be and how he can use it in the fabric he is building."

It has been urged that courage, unfaltering courage, is the primary requisite of a president. However, courage may be manifested in unyielding insistence upon things that are in the highest degree undesirable. A president may stubbornly (and courageously, if you will) demand that the college sacrifice its educational ideals for the sake of securing funds or to please persons of position and influence. In short, courage may prove a curse and a bane, not a blessing, unless it is joined to high university ideals. Undoubtedly, courage is most desirable and valuable provided (but only provided) it is united to true educational leadership.

I was once asked by the president of the Board of Trustees of Stanford University how old a man should be, to be chosen for the presidency of a college. I replied, "That, I think, is one of the least important factors in determining the choice." As an actual fact, in our large institutions it is seldom that a faculty member stands out as a leader, or has been tested as a dean, before he reaches at least the age of forty-five years; he may easily be fifty or fifty-five years old. I see no reason, however, why a person at that age should not be named president. If the institution's age of retirement is sixty-five years, it can look forward to ten or fifteen years of service. Is this not enough? Only one President of the United States has served longer than eight years, and a Constitutional amendment has been proposed, and ratified by the required number of states, limiting the tenure to that period. Assuredly, ten or fifteen years in a college presidency are not too few. Besides, if the president is chosen from among those who have spent their lives in the academic world, he will have far less to learn of his responsibilities and duties than those who are elevated to the Presidency of the United States.

Moreover, is it not a fact that men in new executive posts are often most fertile of new ideas and "shoot their bolt" during their first ten years in office and then not infrequently move "on flat tires" (to change the figure)? They have either succeeded in accomplishing what they sought, or have failed; they may therefore feel content with their achievements or regard their aims as impossible of fulfillment. Of course, exceptions to this generalization may be cited; nonetheless it is often true.

The President

Presumably, trustees like to select a fairly young president so that they can be free from this responsibility for at least two decades, preferably three. This can hardly be regarded, however, as itself a convincing argument for the choice of a very young man.

To be sure, there is the physical vigor and readiness to embark on new projects which young men possess. But assuredly there are many men in their late forties and early fifties who retain both. If not, we have been stupid in choosing Presidents of the United States, for only one of the last ten, Theodore Roosevelt, was less than fifty years of age when he entered upon what is probably the heaviest task any human being can undertake.

And the hope that a new college president may not have to be selected for twenty or twenty-five years is often a vain one, for "the average tenure of the college president, according to a study made some years ago, is less than five years."[6] When Benjamin Ide Wheeler, who eventually served as President of the University of California for a full twenty years, had completed his first fifteen years in the post, he said: "When I came here fifteen years ago I did not expect to be here fifteen years, in the first place because I did not suppose anybody could stay that long. I found out that the average

[6] Oliver C. Carmichael, "What Makes a Good College President," *American Association of University Professors Bulletin*, Vol. 33 (1947), p. 683. Hubert P. Beck, *Men Who Control Our Universities* (New York: King's Crown Press, 1947), p. 203, n. 20, says: "The survey of land-grant colleges and universities reported that '167 presidents of a total of 308 served less than five years.' . . . The average length of service [i.e., of American college and university presidents] is variously stated as 'about five years (Thwing), 9.4 years (Upham), and 9.52 years (Edmiston).' "

term of the office had been three and three-quarters years, and I was perfectly willing to fall in with the usage."

However, it is the stronger institutions in which the president's tenure is the longer. Harvard's Charles W. Eliot served forty years, and Columbia's Nicholas Murray Butler forty-four years. The presidents now in office at California, Harvard, and Princeton, and the recently retired chancellor at Chicago, have all been in office at least fifteen years. Nonetheless, for the chief executive officer to look forward to a term of twenty-five years or more is to hope for what is only occasionally realized.

On the other hand, presidents may last too long. I think the academic world, as a whole, feels that Nicholas Murray Butler, despite his undoubted ability, would have served his university well had he retired earlier than he did. After all, there is a physical side to a president's work. Surely, if an age is set for the retirement of a professor, the president should retire no later—probably earlier. Besides, a president will have sought to introduce whatever he thinks wise during his first—or even his second—decade; after that, his effort is often directed toward keeping things placid— toward letting the boat merely glide on its way. And the octogenarian president is thus likely, whenever any supposedly new suggestion is made, to point out that this or something like it was tried long years before and proved a failure. Moreover, too long a service on the president's part may make him the more opinionated, the less likely to take advice. He may easily feel that his experience is so great, in fact so much greater than that of his faculty, and of course so much more extensive, that he will tend to believe himself well-nigh omniscient.

From every point of view, the most important and difficult task that trustees have is the choice of a president. And they should be particularly careful to secure the counsel of the faculty before they act. The consultation should be with a considerable number of the faculty, as well as with a small selected committee. It must be remembered that professors will usually be able to give valuable information about those on their own and other faculties who are proposed for appointment; they will know both the strength and the weaknesses of those men as no trustee is likely to know them. Moreover, faculty members can give their judgment of the likelihood that a candidate suggested will fit into the presidency of that particular institution. When a president is elected by the trustees in secret session immediately after a vacancy occurs, and without a conference with the faculty, it can safely be said that there has been political manipulation and that the choice is one that the faculty, in all probability, would not have approved.

In any event, the choice of a president might well be entered upon with prayer, since the decision will in large measure determine the future of the institution for weal or woe.

III.
The Trustees

THE FINAL AUTHORITY

All power is a trust.

DISRAELI, *Vivian Grey*

THE OFFICIAL governing board of a college or university consists of trustees or, if the institution is publicly supported, regents. Legally, they have complete and absolute control of the college, save so far as state constitutions or articles of incorporation may limit or restrict them.

Such a body is in our country clearly indispensable; if the faculty were to be the ultimate governors, there would be lacking that bond between society and the college which is essential. It is especially necessary that the public which supports a state or municipal institution be thus represented, in order that the college may not be estranged from the people. On the other hand, it is equally necessary that the faculty be given sole authority over academic matters, such as curricula, courses, admission requirements, and the like; otherwise the character of the institution may be radically altered and its standards greatly lowered. The faculty must both set these up and administer them, and the college will suffer seriously if the trustees in any way seek to deal with them. The trustees should determine the major policies of the institution and should not serve merely as rubber stamps for the president, and the latter should be held responsible by them for the administration of the policies they have determined. They should not surrender their proper functions; but it is a fact to be remembered that, "having selected the president, they usually leave the current management of the institution to him and the faculty."[1]

It is most important that the trustees understand what is meant by academic freedom and resolutely protect the members of the faculty in the frank expression of their views in the classroom, the lecture halls, or in publication. A university would cease to be worthy of the name if its faculty were muzzled. They are not employees in the ordinary sense of the term, and must not be treated as if they were. A striking instance of failure to understand this was revealed in the academic difficulties at the University of Texas which led finally to the regents' dismissal of the president, Dr. Homer P. Rainey. A report of a committee of the American Association of University Professors is very direct and fundamental: "Statements made by these regents to the representatives of the Association make it clear that they regard this relationship [i.e., of the regents to the president and the faculty] to be that of a private employer to his employees, a relationship in which the Regents are not debarred by any moral restrictions beyond their own individual sense of expediency from imposing their personal views and prejudices upon the teaching of the University and from employing the power of dismissal to gratify their private antipathies and resentments. They have made

---

[1] Abraham Flexner, *Universities, American, English, German* (Oxford University Press, 1930), p. 179.

it clear that they regard the University of Texas as a proprietary institution. . . . Any university that suppresses or seeks to suppress academic freedom proclaims to the public that it is a proprietary institution, and the public should be so advised to the end that steps may be taken to regain for that institution its educational character."[2]

Nothing therefore is more important, absolutely nothing, in the appointment of trustees than that men be chosen who understand clearly the nature of the university and the function of its faculty. They must protect the right of the members of the faculty to express themselves with complete frankness, against all who may seek to restrain them, be they a governor, a legislature, alumni, donors, or the general public. The air of freedom must, without fail, blow through academic halls.[3]

The term for which trustees are chosen should be long—at least eight years; in this way they come to know the institution in its complexities and can really render service. For public institutions the power of appointment should be vested wholly in the chief executive of the state or the city. This obviously does not guarantee success in the selection of the trustees; but what human system can? There is the obvious danger that the appointments may be political, and as a result political influences may be introduced into the board. This depends entirely upon the kind of man the people have elected as governor. Yet any requirement of approval of such nominations by a legislative body

[2] *AAUP Bulletin,* Vol. 30 (1944), pp. 629–630.

[3] The motto of Stanford University is: *Die Luft der Freiheit weht* ("The Winds of Freedom Blow").

exposes them to still additional political influence and certainly weakens responsibility.

The regents of public institutions are at times chosen by popular election, as for example at Nebraska, Illinois, and Michigan. But many men of a type most valuable to board membership would decline to submit their names to the electorate. Some of those who would run for the office might seek to make improper use of the position. Besides, to expect men to spend money campaigning for a post that carries no salary and should carry none is assuredly absurd and illogical. As a whole, persons named by gubernatorial appointments have been individually satisfactory, save of course when the state selects a poor governor.

A great danger in the selection of trustees is that they will all come from the same stratum of society, so to speak: they will be chosen because they are well known or because they are rich. If they are rich men, there is the scarcely disguised hope that either they will generously pour money into the college's coffers or at least be able to get it from their wealthy associates. This means, of course, that in considering such questions as come before them, including amount of tuition fees, cost of dormitories, and the like, they may neglect the interests of students with modest resources. After all, society—and it is society which in reality supports a college, whether it be a state university or an independent institution—has as its aims the providing of higher education for those who are worthy of it and who will render the greatest service to the community. Many a widow's mite has come to a college—and assuredly the donor would not wish students of humble means ignored. And at times a wealthy donor, recalling his rise from poverty, wishes to help others obtain the education for which he had to struggle or which perhaps he was unable to secure.

The attitude revealed by some rich trustees in giving slight consideration to the students whose purses are slender appears in not a few matters, great and small. The only way to meet this situation is to see to it that appointments are made from all strata of society. Men of moderate means should be chosen; persons from the ranks of labor should by all means be included. From the loins of such as these may come sons and daughters in whom the college will in later years take the greatest pride.

There is the further danger that trustees will be ultraconservative in their point of view and seek to secure conformity to the opinions they hold. These are primarily the opinions held by the business and banking element of society. Boards of trustees of private colleges are especially subject to this danger. The need they almost invariably have for additional funds naturally leads them to make such appointments. Then too, the board, filling its own vacancies, becomes a sort of club, and when new trustees are to be chosen the question of fitting in with the group is often in mind, though not always expressed.

If our colleges are to render their highest service, they must not be class institutions, either in their student body or in their governing board. This need becomes greatest when a new president is to be chosen. As he is to be the head of an institution, intended to minister to truth, the utmost care must be taken that he is not selected because he belongs to a certain group or has ingratiated himself with its members. On the other hand, it must be recalled that, save for the choice of a president, among the most important functions of the board are those relating to finance and the physical side of the institution. It is therefore highly desirable, indeed essential, that its membership shall include able financiers competent to look after the college's investments wisely.

In some colleges there has developed a practice which appears well worth following. The board membership includes one or two who are members of college faculties. They are not members of the local faculty, for there would be too much danger of an assumption that their views represented those of the faculty as a whole. Moreover, self-interest and the interest of the departments or schools of which they were members might, even though unconsciously, color their decisions. No; the faculty members should be selected from other institutions, preferably those of the same type. They leaven the point of view of the board and help keep its course directed to the educational purposes of the college. The president may well find them most valuable aids when he presents a recommendation which is drawn from his own close contact with the institution, but which many board members are unable to see in proper perspective. The faculty of the college itself has sometimes enjoyed the privilege of electing a board member from the faculty of a sister institution; but there is the possibility that a person so chosen may consider that he has an obligation to represent the faculty which elected him, and will uphold its views. Another, and preferable, procedure is that the governor (or, if the institution is a private one, the trustees), after obtaining from the faculty of the college, and otherwise, all possible light upon desirable and available candidates, shall choose as trustees persons from the list thus prepared.[4]

A difficulty occurs among college trustees, as in many another board membership, because the real business is properly performed by subcommittees and the board meeting tends to be confined to the perfunctory approval of committee reports. There are various devices by which this can be somewhat obviated. Visits on the day of board meetings to a particular building of the campus and thorough inspection of it can readily be arranged; at the same time, accounts of the work going on in it, and indeed the work of that department as a whole, can properly be given by appropriate faculty members. Another device is to place on the agenda some important general questions, not so much for action at that time as to stimulate thought and further study by the board members; for example, To what ultimate size of student body should the institution look forward? The appropriate officials could present data bearing on the matter and including figures from other institutions.

I have urged that trustees be given terms of eight years or more. The common practice by which the terms of members expire in rotation is excellent; this means that there is some "turnover" in the board at the end of each year, and yet continuity of policy can be maintained. If the term of office is very long, it is wise not to permit reappointment; otherwise, new blood may not be brought into the board. Each trustee prizing the honor will expect or seek renewal of his ap-

[4] Cf. Alan Reynolds Thompson, "The Professor and the Governing Board," *AAUP Bulletin*, Vol. 35 (1949), pp. 678–687.

pointment. The board will tend to be made up of aged men and women;[5] as a result they may not be accessible to new ideas or procedures. It must be remembered that the institutions they govern are designed to serve youth. If the trustees are alumni, they may place the college of their own undergraduate days on a pedestal as the ideal college and resent any changes whatsoever. Some colleges provide that when a trustee has served his full term, at least a year must elapse before he may again be chosen. This has certain advantages but still does not completely free the institution from the pressure for reappointment.

It has been proposed that there be a regulation forbidding any person of more than a stated age (65 or 70 years) be named a trustee.[6] Since there will naturally be quite a number who, though short of that age at the time of appointment, reach or pass it before completing their full term, the rule proposed will not accomplish the purpose intended. For example, a person appointed a year or two before reaching the "deadline" would be very old when his term expired. Far better would it be to provide that at a definite age (be it 70 years or less) the appointment must cease; this would make it certain that no persons over the stipulated age would serve on the board.

[5] Hubert P. Beck, *Men Who Control Our Universities* (New York: King's Crown Press, 1947), pp. 84–85: of the trustees of the leading thirty universities, "only 4 per cent . . . were under 40 and only 22 per cent under 50 . . . 47 per cent were 60 or over."

[6] "Under the Chicago [i.e., University of Chicago] regulations members of the governing board retire from active status at the age of 70 and become honorary trustees, having the right to attend meetings and participate, as well as to serve on standing committees, but not the privilege of voting or holding office." *Ibid.*, p. 42.

The situation is at its worst when trustees are appointed for life. It is astonishing to learn that at many of our leading institutions some or all of the board members have life tenure. To be sure, there have been admirable trustees who have passed seventy by many years—yes, even eighty,—but these exceptions prove the desirability of some kind of rule. The problems that are presented to the board and that must be settled at a brief meeting are often critical ones for the institution, and require the clearest of minds. And it is tragic to see a trustee, formerly an able member of the board, gradually through age become only a vote, quite unable himself to attack the questions before the body as a whole.

President-Emeritus Raymond M. Hughes of Iowa State College expresses himself vigorously on this entire problem: "In most boards there are too many old men. The average age of the members of a given board is very often too high. It would seem desirable to keep the average age between fifty and sixty. It would also seem desirable that no member should serve beyond the age of seventy years. There should certainly be a substantial number of members between thirty and fifty on these boards.

"It seems more important that the board should be young enough to sense the needs of the people they represent and guide the changing institutions to their largest service, rather than that a large majority of aged men should maintain policies unchanged."[7]

Several foundations have found it desirable to set the age of retirement for their trustees at sixty-five

---

[7] *A Manual for Trustees of Colleges and Universities* (Iowa State College Press, 1945), pp. 6–7.

years, and it is argued that there is no essential difference between their functions and those of collegiate boards. However, in view of clearly justifiable exceptions, it seems unwise to make a specific regulation; rather should the appointing power take into account this factor of age and make it a general principle that the average age of the board shall not go above fifty or fifty-five years at the very highest.

On the other hand, a trustee, whether of a public or a private institution, should not be removable by anyone whatsoever, except for proved malfeasance, immorality, or complete mental incapacity. Governors have sometimes had the power and have removed trustees or regents, usually for the sake of dominating the board and removing the president. This is an outrageous situation and should never be tolerated. Regents should be chosen for set terms, and the governor should be denied the power of removal save for the causes already cited, and then only after a fair and public trial. If he were to request a resignation before the regent's term had expired, the request should be emphatically refused. The regent should realize that in declining to resign he is not merely protecting his own position, but is protecting the entire board against the illegal and improper usurpation of power by the governor. The purpose in staggering the terms of members of a board is to prevent any one governor from dominating it, and acquiescence in his request for a resignation would completely defeat the intent of the people as expressed in the state constitution.

It is even more important for the trustees to support the president and not even to dream of removing him save for flagrant failure to perform his duties or for immoral conduct, and then there should be a fair trial at which the president would have the fullest of opportunities to present his defense. Such scandals as that at the University of Texas spring from abuse of the power of regents and a complete misconception of the nature and purpose of a university; it is usually due to a desire to muzzle the president or the faculty and to deny them the freedom that is imperatively necessary in an institution of higher learning.

Appropriations for state institutions must, of course, come from the legislature; but its grants should be total grants; the legislature should have no authority to pass upon individual items, whether sums allocated for particular departments or schools, or salaries of faculty or administrative staff. Legislatures have enough and more than enough to do without deciding whether Economics shall receive such and such a sum, or whether Professor X shall have his salary increased. Besides, legislators are not chosen because of their competence to decide which department should receive additional funds. I fear too that Agriculture would receive the lion's share, while Art and French would have hard sledding. The authority to vote the precise budget should be vested wholly in the regents or trustees, but they too should refrain from determining individual items. This must be the president's responsibility after careful consideration of the needs of the various departments. The standing orders or by-laws of the institution should make crystal-clear the procedure involved in preparing and adopting the budget.

It is particularly important that the board never interfere as a whole or individually in the appointment of a member of the faculty or his promotion. Here too we have a matter that is wholly academic, and while formal action must be taken by the board, the responsibility should always be the president's, who in turn must previously secure the recommendation both of the department concerned and of an appropriate faculty committee.

In the year 1899, Benjamin Ide Wheeler was elected President of the University of California. He wrote the Regents a brief letter setting forth the terms on which he would accept. It happened that shortly before this a member of the faculty whose promotion to the grade of associate professor had been opposed by the chairman of his department and by the President was nevertheless advanced in rank by the Regents. Gossip had it that a Regent who was a cousin of his had exerted influence on his behalf. At any rate, with this incident in mind, Dr. Wheeler demanded that the initiative in all appointments, promotions, demotions, and dismissals should be vested in the President. And it was on these terms that he accepted. This did not mean that the Regents had to accept all the recommendations; they still had the power to reject any proposals made. But they were at no time to appoint, promote, or dismiss unless the President had submitted such a recommendation.

It frequently happens that trustees do not really know the institution which they are governing. As a group, and far more as individuals, they should be encouraged to visit it often, to meet at times with student groups, and more often with the faculty. This will make the college something other than a column of figures or a map of the grounds. It will make each body understand better the point of view of the other, and each will see the other as a group of human beings eager to do the best possible for the institution. They will cease to be that vague, far-off thing *The Trustees*, or that supposedly impractical body *The Faculty*. An annual dinner of trustees and faculty is admirable; it will break the ice and the barriers.

It is good if some of the trustees, at least, make their university connection their primary activity aside from their business or profession. By merely walking about the grounds they will see things that can and should be done. So too, frequent contacts with professors and students are good. But the trustee must nonetheless refrain, on the basis of such information, from pressing action on the board in matters falling properly under the authority of the president or the faculty. When he sees a problem and believes he sees also a solution to it, he may properly offer his solution to the president in private conversation for the latter's consideration, and then leave it in his hands.

Assuredly one would hope that quite a number of alumni should be designated as regents, but there is no reason why any official or officials of their formal organization should have seats on the board. In other words, alumni should be chosen on the basis of their individual desirability as regents.

Unquestionably, women should be named to the board of a state institution. There should not be merely a token appointment of one woman only; the board need not be equally divided between men and women, but surely a certain number of women are entitled to places on the governing body of an institution which educates women as well as men. At women's colleges there should be a large proportion of women on the board; but men are needed too, for the supervision of finances, approval of building plans, and the like. In general, however, the principles laid down for trustees are equally applicable to those in charge of women's colleges and of men's.

Every effort should be made to keep board meetings from degenerating to little more than perfunctory approval of committee reports; some problem of importance to the institution should be placed before every meeting. The president may bring in a number of faculty members specially concerned with the particular topic and able to enlighten the board on the faculty point of view.

Far more important than anything else is the character of the man or woman appointed to the board. "Real devotion to the cause of education, profound concern for the public good, sterling integrity, courage to face pressure, political and otherwise, fearlessly— these qualities combined with high intelligence and some knowledge of higher education should be prerequisites to the consideration of a man or woman for appointment."[8]

It is extraordinary how swiftly a change may develop in a board, especially when external pressure exists or is feared. Men's devotion to university ideals is really tested when an issue arises on which a considerable segment of the public feels strongly. When I spoke at a meeting of the National Association of State Universities in May, 1949, I said that I felt there was no university in the country where the relations

---

[8] Raymond M. Hughes, *A Manual for Trustees of Colleges and Universities* (Iowa State College Press, 1945), p. 7.

between the administration and the faculty were as good as those at the University of California. And immediately thereafter came the more than two years of conflict beginning with the proposal to establish a loyalty oath. Subsequently, the oath was embodied in a contract, with the alternative of a faculty committee hearing; certain members of the faculty who declined to sign were dismissed by the Regents, but the Appellate Court of the Third District unanimously ordered their reinstatement. The case has now been taken over by the Supreme Court of the State. At the time this book appears, no decision has yet been made by the Court; moreover, no report has yet been issued by the American Association of University Professors, to which an appeal was made. In any event, great harm has been done the University. Not only have members of the faculty who possessed tenure and were established as not Communists been dismissed; others have resigned in protest, a number of scholars invited to join the faculty on one or another of the University's campuses have declined, and the morale of the faculty has suffered severely. In the light of my own relation to the University, it seems inappropriate to go into further detail.

It is but fair to say that throughout the land hundreds (nay, thousands) of men and women are conscientiously rendering excellent service as trustees of colleges, great and small. They are giving untold hours to board meetings and committee meetings, frequently traveling many miles for this purpose. They are generously sacrificing time that they cannot well withdraw from their other duties. And they are making it possible for many a college to rest upon a sound financial foundation. After all, while there is honor in such a post, this by no means makes up for the energy spent. It is through a genuine interest in the institutions themselves that these men and women devote so much time and thought to their well-being.

IV.
Public Relations

A blast of that dread horn.

SCOTT, Marmion

ONE OF THE most obvious respects in which our colleges have yielded to the practices of the business world is in the matter of public relations. Certainly, the achievements of the university and its faculty, their researches and publications, any recognition given them, any new programs of study, the accomplishments of such of its alumni as have attained distinction—these and similar matters should come to the attention of the community. But all too often, since the field of public relations is in the hands of men who have previously been engaged in advertising or newspaper work, those items are played up which are most likely to command the largest popular interest, while that which from a scholarly point of view is far more important is either overlooked entirely or given a decidedly minor place. Indeed, even academic matters or discoveries are all too often described with the kind of headlines that will catch the eye of the public at the expense of the distortion or vulgarization of the subject matter.

A university should not cheapen itself by utilizing to any degree the methods of the yellow press. The public should take the institution for what it is, not as

44

it may be portrayed in lurid colors. To be sure, the account will have to be written in terms that the man on the street can understand, but this does not call for a false or exaggerated picture.

Moreover, the term "public relations" is at times so stretched that it embraces far more territory than the dissemination of news concerning the college. It may be construed to include such matters as these: Who should be invited to deliver a lecture on the campus? What reply should be made to an attack on the institution? What invitations to speak, to join organizations, to become an official of a society, or the like, should the president accept? Who should represent the college at a particular academic function or gathering? To be sure, in a certain sense all these matters do concern the relations of the college to the public. But if one is so inclined, "public relations" can be expanded to include a vastly wider range. The choice of trustees to fill vacancies, for example, is assuredly of very great concern to the public. But if one were to accept this principle to the fullest degree, the person at the head of the department of public relations becomes almost as important as the president, certainly more important than any dean. And since he is chosen because of his experience and skill in the newspaper or advertising field, such power concentrated in his hands is a great danger to the institution. Scholarly ideals may well be subordinated to the bombastic, the striking, the noisy, or to political expediency. University publicity would then not seek to give a true picture of the work of the college, but to portray it in the way that is thought to be most appealing to the general public. The number of students becomes more important than the quality of the faculty, athletic supremacy far exceeds intellectual. And when the field of public relations is so expanded, the atmosphere of the market place tends to fill almost every nook and corner of the campus. John Doe must not be invited to speak because he will offend the labor organizations, William Smith is anathema to the National Association of Manufacturers, Roger Benton is unwelcome because he is an Anglophobe, Otto Robinson is a bit too "pink." Fear and cowardice will govern all decisions, and an institution pledged to seek and teach the truth will sell its birthright in the hope of securing a mess of pottage.

"Public relations" is a term which should be abolished in college halls. Let the institution have a news bureau, but a modest one. It does not take a horde of reporters to let the public know what the institution is really doing. Then those activities which the octopus of public relations has grasped within its tentacles can fall under the jurisdiction of appropriate academic officials, not reporters masquerading as important university officers. And whatever publicity is sent out should first be read with care by some collegiate official, with an eye not only to its accuracy, but also its fidelity to the highest university ideals.

It may be argued that there are numerous matters, not falling under the term "news," which properly concern the external relations of the institution. There certainly are. Often the president himself, or the vice-president, will consider the matter important enough to handle personally. Otherwise, they should be delegated to appropriate academic officials. If the relations with agricultural interests are involved, who would more appropriately deal with them than the dean of the college of agriculture? If there is the possibility of a gift toward a new dormitory, the chairman of the dormitory committee would be a fitting university representative. When the problems are legal, the attorney for the trustees should, of course, act.

In any event, the department called Public Relations should have its wings clipped, and the matters which now fall under its jurisdiction should be referred to academic officials who will handle them primarily from the point of view of the university as an educational institution. Obviously, when action is likely to follow, the president's approval should be sought.

V.
The Deans

I have done the state some service, and they know 't.

Othello

D EANS perform a large part of the administrative work of colleges and universities, that is, what may be called the academic administrative work, as distinguished from purely financial operations, care of the grounds, and the like. They are the officials in charge of the various academic units of the institutions. There are deans of graduate schools, of colleges of liberal arts (or letters and science), agriculture, pharmacy, dentistry, and schools of medicine, law, business administration, librarianship, social service, and so on. These men carry great responsibilities for the work in their particular segments of the institution. Sometimes, indeed, it would be far better if they were given still greater authority than they have, thereby relieving the central administration (the president's office) of some of the countless matters which pour in upon it, on many of which, moreover, the deans must in any event be consulted.

The dean should, of course, be a capable administrator; he should be ready to decide matters and not keep them in an "either . . . or" status. Naturally, his decision should be based on a careful investigation of all the facts involved. But when he has done so, he

48

should give a "Yes" or "No," and the decision made should stick.

The deans' authority should be very extensive in their own area; the president should delegate it to the utmost possible degree and in explicit terms. They should, for example, have primary responsibility for making up the budgets of their schools or colleges. They should have final jurisdiction with reference to appointments and promotions to all posts save those granting permanent tenure, and in reference to these their recommendations should carry the greatest weight. They should be *ex officio* members of all standing committees in their units, and should be responsible for initiating changes in curricula and for passing upon courses acceptable for degrees. These are but illustrations of the power I believe should be granted to deans.

On the other hand, there is often danger of excessive multiplication of deans. Whenever those engaged in a particular curriculum, especially a new field like journalism or criminology, wish to add to its dignity, they propose that it be made a school or college with a dean at its head. Frequently it would be better, so far as quality of work is concerned, if this fledgling curriculum were retained in an already established college and held to its often more exacting standards; this would at least prevent specialization from being carried altogether too far.

By delegating large authority to deans, two highly important results will be accomplished. In the first place, decisions can be made far more promptly than if they have to go through "channels" to the president's desk and wait in competition with a multitude of other and frequently more important problems. Besides, since the dean will constantly deal with matters in his field of authority, he will at once know the issues involved and be likely to act far more consistently; and on the other hand, the president will be freed from a host of minor burdens and be able to devote himself to matters of primary importance to the institution.

Moreover, is it not best that the president should not be "the All-powerful," from whose lips fall decisions on matters small as well as great? Is not an institution better served when power is not too highly concentrated, and a large degree of authority rests with men close to the problems concerned and likely to be able to give far more time to discuss them with their colleagues? Thereby the president's time and thought are reserved for those problems on which he and he alone should make the final decision.

A dean should be willing to accept the fact that the successful administrator of an important part of an institution must be willing, while so serving, to make sacrifices in the field of scholarship. The post almost always involves an abandonment of at least some of one's scholarly aims. A few deans have fully or almost fully continued their scholarly careers—possibly through failure to do their duty by the deanship. On the other hand, a deanship should be assigned only to a man whose scholarship has won the respect of his colleagues; otherwise, they may be reluctant to follow his lead in academic matters and, indeed, will distrust his actions in reference to appointments and promotions.

He should be willing to give unlimited time to conferences, both with members of the faculty and with students. (One dean has described his functions to me as those of a janitor, alluding to his caring for endless minor matters and being, as it were, at the beck and call of the faculty.) He needs tact in dealing with his colleagues; he should of course use the aid of various committees, made up of faculty members of recognized judgment and standing, and should test his proposals in committee before submitting them to the faculty as a whole. In the same way, the deans themselves should meet at intervals to deal with matters of overlapping jurisdiction and topics that affect them all. To such a group it is desirable to add faculty leaders who are not deans, for the faculty believes—sometimes correctly—that a dean loses the "common touch" and looks upon university problems from the point of view of (shall I say?) a governing class.

The faculty has mingled feelings toward deans, in part a feeling of respect and a recognition of the influence they exert in university matters, in part a certain scorn because of the numerous petty matters with which they must deal and their abandonment of a scholarly career in favor of administration. A favorite faculty jest is: "A dean is too smart to be a president and not smart enough to be a professor."

An exceedingly important and difficult question relates to the tenure of deans. Should they serve for stipulated terms (say five years) and then be ineligible for reappointment, reverting to the status of professors? Should they serve one such term and be eligible for reappointment for a second term, but no more? Should they be appointed for a set term (one or more years) but be eligible for indefinite reappointments, so that they may become in effect permanent officials?

If the limit of tenure is five years, men may hesitate to accept the post, realizing that at its close they will resume the professorship and meanwhile have lost five years of productive scholarship, and that too at an age, perhaps, when they would shrink from sacrificing so large a fraction of the active years ahead of them. If the limit, according to the second alternative, is ten years, the case becomes even more serious, since at the end of ten years spent in activities remote from research the professor will probably find it well-nigh impossible to "get into his stride" again.

Should we, then, think of the third suggestion and assume that if the incumbent "makes good" he will hold the post permanently or at least indefinitely? There is much to say for this. The number of men in any professional field qualified to serve as deans, and willing to do so, is limited, and if a thoroughly competent man can be found, why not hold fast to him? Besides, administration runs more smoothly when there is continuity of supervision.

There arises once more the question of the sacrifice, on the part of deans, of their careers as scholars. It would be unfair to demand this sacrifice from a group of men in a faculty; it is bad enough that it seems required of the president. The best solution unquestionably is to provide so much assistance to a dean, in the form of assistant deans, secretaries, and clerks, that he can confine himself to questions of policy, to unprecedented issues, and to problems that involve borderline decisions. Such assistance and, if necesary, a reduction in his teaching load, will make it possible for him, even though he is a dean, to continue in some degree his scholarly work.

Certainly all needed aid should be given him; but at the same time there is danger that the staff of secretaries and clerks—indeed the entire nonacademic staff—may be expanded more and more, thereby diverting from the more important functions of the university the funds that they urgently require. Every effort should be made to simplify rules so that time may not be required for the scrutinizing of piles of petitions for special exceptions to rules. The general rules should be both simple and clear, and unless a student asks something extraordinary, the according or denying of exceptional treatment should reside wholly in the hands of the assistant dean or even of an experienced administrative assistant. In some places the dean is forced to carry far too many burdens, act upon too many routine matters, and supply information that others can give equally well. His main function should be to strengthen the academic work of his school or college, find its weaknesses and seek to remove them, and take note of the best teachers and scholars and give them help and encouragement.

No man should be made a dean unless the president really has confidence in him, and this confidence should be shown by his constantly calling upon the dean for counsel and advice in matters within his area of competence. And so long as he has the president's confidence and, no less, that of his colleagues, he should continue as dean, unless of course the duties become irksome or he wishes to gain release so that he may devote himself single-mindedly to scholarship.

Save for the most burdensome deanships, the posts should be held by men who still retain professorial titles and do some teaching and research. In that way they will keep in touch at first hand with the two primary university functions, and not be tempted to look upon record keeping and other like administrative tasks as of most importance. They should be professors as well as deans and not leave their professorships to enter into a new and, as they may think, superior realm.

American society often pays more respect to the title "dean" than it deserves. To be sure, some deans have done much for their schools or colleges in beating new trails or improving the quality of work done, but others merely keep the office going and administer the established rules. Of course, those who really contribute to the development or advancement of their schools or colleges deserve our utmost respect since they are performing a highly important task and making a lasting contribution to the intellectual life of the institution. And such men should take pride in both the name and the service they render as deans.

After spending twenty-eight years of my university life as an administrative officer, I often ask myself whether I would do it again if I had my life to live over. In spite of my natural and genuine regret that my scholarly opportunities were first reduced and later completely removed, I believe I should be willing to do exactly what I have done. To be sure, my shelf has no long rows of volumes which I have written, and my bibliography in more recent years contains not even scholarly articles. Yet I venture to hope that somehow I have left something at least in the institution through my efforts, and I am cheered by the recollection of my contacts with my colleagues and with the successive generations of students and the thought that I have been able to give at least some help to individual professors and students now and then.

It has been my good fortune to go on with my administrative work till the end of the trail. However, I feel deep regret for men who give years of service as administrative officers and then, as the result of a change in a presidency, fail to receive reappointment. To pick up the threads of scholarly work when the day of retirement is close at hand is extremely difficult and discouraging. And this is unquestionably the hazard to which a man exposes himself if he embarks on an administrative career.

VI.
The Faculty

THEY REALLY MAKE THE INSTITUTION

And gladly wolde he lerne, and gladly teche.
CHAUCER, Canterbury Tales

W E MAY TALK as we please of authority and power in a college, emphasizing the position of trustees, president, and deans, but nonetheless the basic work of the institution is done by the faculty. The others stand in the limelight; they are assumed by the public to be the college—but they are not. Everything that makes an institution of higher learning springs from the faculty. It is they who carry on research, pushing forward the boundaries of knowledge in every field of scholarship represented in the institution. It is they who keep in constant touch with the advances in their specialties made by scholars in the other universities of the world; were it not for this, the published learning of a scientist in one college would command no audience, leave no impress on the accepted knowledge of the subject on which he has been working. And it is they who instruct the students who flock to our colleges; they guide students in their studies and research and inspire a following generation of teachers and scholars. They too are the ones who equip men and women to pursue successfully the manifold professions of the modern world—medicine, law, dentistry, engineering, and a host of others. And, by no means least, they train students to use their minds, to make thoughtful judgments—in short, to become intelligent human beings, whatever their lifework may be.

What is there of real significance in an institution of higher learning save these activities? Surely everything else is intended to make it possible for the professor to carry them on more successfully. New buildings, new studies, new laboratories, additional books, more equipment—what are these but the means by which scholars work and teach the better? Of course, there are financial accounts, record keeping, disciplining of students, caring for roads and traffic, policing the grounds, and a multitude of other activities, useful and necessary but unquestionably subordinate to the primary functions of the institution, which are instruction and research.

If one were asked to describe the ideal teacher in college or university, the result would, I fear, be a wholly unrealizable picture. He should of course be well grounded in his field and have shown at least that minimum of scholarship represented by his degree of Doctor of Philosophy or its equivalent. However, he should not be a man who has "learned more and more about less and less"; although he has written a dissertation on one particular and definite topic, his knowledge in his field of study should be broad and extensive. The doctoral dissertation should be merely the first step in his research activity; he should not rest upon it as the ultimate crest of the hill to be surmounted, but as merely the first mile of the ascent. He should enlarge his field of special interest so that it is far broader than his work for the doctorate.

However, his interests should by no means be confined to the department in which he teaches; he should remember that the world is full of many things that are of importance to us all. The scientist should be concerned with works of letters; the professor of English should not be blind to the accomplishments of science; and neither should be unaware of national and international problems. In short, the teacher should be a well-educated person, and he will unquestionably discover that there is an interrelation between various fields of knowledge that will often throw light on the specific problems with which he is wrestling.

But he should be a teacher as well as a scholar. He should be interested in teaching, and concerned with devising the most effective methods of presentation; he should, I trust, think of students as individuals and be not only willing but eager to discuss with them both questions pertaining to the particular course and those having to do with their college careers and even problems of a personal nature. Though students often speak of their instructors in a somewhat disparaging tone, in their hearts they respect them and have regard for their judgment.

The teacher should be concerned with the problems of his department and of the college as a whole. He should attend departmental and faculty meetings regularly and be ready in season to serve patiently and carefully upon their committees. He should have cultural interests and attend the best plays, concerts, and operas, and not hold aloof from lectures by his colleagues, even in fields of study remote from his own. He should remember that a college is not an institution existing in a vacuum, but a part of American society. He should be willing (so far as it does not hamper his primary responsibilities) to lecture in his own field to clubs and societies which may be interested. It is good, too, if he makes himself a member of civic organizations and keeps in touch with his fellow citizens who are not professors. All these things will make him a better-rounded and assuredly a more successful teacher. They will even aid his research, as placing in better perspective the work which he is doing; he will see the difference between potty, run-of-the-mill research and that broader type which should bring results not merely useful but illuminating.

And by no means least should be that intangible thing called personality. Teachers who possess it will leave with their students something that will abide with them all their lives. It is not a pleasant manner or a series of amusing stories. It is character, as expressed by the instructor in the day-by-day work of the course. It makes the subject matter more significant. Far more than that, it helps to shape the thoughts and actions of the student. Yet such a person as I have depicted is rare indeed; he is, I know, the ideal, not the real.

If, however, I were asked, "Of all these qualities, which would you place first and foremost?" I should unhesitatingly reply, "Scholarship, personality, and success in teaching." All too often, research is thought of as frosting on the cake of the college. It is far more than that. Scholarly work keeps the teacher alive in his own field; he is not merely repeating in altered words what is to be found in textbooks. To be sure, he cannot be carrying on research in all fields in which he teaches courses; but the attitude toward learning derived from actually continuing research will inevitably show itself in his teaching. And in advanced courses such as graduate seminars I should never want a person to be teaching unless he had delved deeply into the specific field. Research not only does not harm the teacher; it makes him a better teacher. He is engaged in striving to arrive at irrefutable conclusions on a particular problem and seeks to present his own arguments concerning the special topic with the utmost cogency. And through doing such work his entire attitude toward the myriad of problems which will arise in his teaching, but which he cannot pursue with the same thoroughness, will be affected. He becomes imbued with the methods of scholarship because he applies them constantly and thus is able to draw sounder conclusions on disputed topics.

Yet there are some men whose interest in research is such that they ought not to teach. They should be members of research institutions, for then they can devote themselves wholly to investigation. Teaching, save for guiding a few chosen souls in their own special field, makes no appeal to them, and it is a mistake to entrust classes to them. But they are few; and even so, they are capable of making such great contributions to human knowledge as to merit special accommodation in our universities.

Assuredly, college teaching is one of the noblest of activities. And American society seems to believe in education; at least, on any and all occasions public speakers and writers of editorials praise it in eloquent words. But it must be confessed that these words by no means always result in action. The position of the teacher is not held in the highest esteem; he is certainly regarded by the public as greatly inferior to the lawyer, the physician, the officer in the army or navy the successful business executive, and many another member of society. Even the college professor by no means receives the same regard as is manifested toward his colleagues in European lands. Of course, if an "expert" in a particular field is required, a professor may be called on, but otherwise he is considered a strange fish engaged in an occupation inferior to the truly manly ones. You recall the old saying: "Those who can, do; those who can't, teach." Many of us remember how, when Woodrow Wilson ran for President, he was scornfully depicted as clad in academic dress with a mortarboard perched askew on his head.

And it is this attitude, not the sugared public utterances, which leads to the inadequate salaries paid to college teachers. Stop to think what this means. The young man who has spent four years as an undergraduate in college then goes on to the graduate school. He almost never obtains his Ph.D. in less than three years; often it is five or seven. Then, if he is fortunate, he secures an instructorship at $2,700 per annum;[1] he is a man of 27 or 29 years and probably married. The gravediggers in San Francisco were not long ago on a strike because they were being paid but $12 per day; they won the strike and were gradually advanced to $12.50 per day. I do not mean that gravediggers are receiving too much; most of them have families to support. But men with the years of training of a college teacher and, above all, engaged in an occupation so

[1] *AAUP Bulletin,* Vol. 33 (1947), p. 450: "The median of all the minimum salaries of instructors was found to be $2,000" in 1946–47. In 1949–50 it was apparently about $2,700; cf. *AAUP Bulletin,* Vol. 35 (1949), pp. 734–747.

important to society should certainly be receiving a far greater remuneration.

Besides, most of those who become teachers come from families of very modest means. As a result, the prospective college teacher has had to divert part (often a considerable part) of his time and thought to earning money for self-support. This has delayed the receipt of the doctorate; frequently it has made it necessary for him to borrow funds in order to meet expenses. Hence he begins his service as a teacher with a debt hanging over him, and must set aside each month a part of his small salary toward paying his obligations. And even if the latter is not the case, the young teacher should be in such a financial position that he need not worry about money, but can devote himself with all his mind and thought to his university obligations. He should not have to eke out his salary by seeking outside lecture engagements, teaching extension classes, or even giving courses in a neighboring college.

Picture the present situation of Instructor Smith, a young man who is intellectually among the ablest of his college mates, goes on to spend four or five years in advanced study, and ultimately wins the degree of Doctor. After careful investigation he is selected by a college as the kind of man desired for the faculty as teacher and scholar. What then? He is in a state of constant worry over how he will meet his expenses, make both ends meet. He has to write potboilers or spend hours in giving extra lectures to add to his meager salary. His excellent mind, which should be concentrated on his teaching, his students, and his scholarly work, is distracted by worry and by extraneous, moneymaking activities. This is not deriving the full measure of profit from the young man's talent or giving him a fair chance to make the most of himself. It is not the way to make great scholars or great teachers. The instructor's minimum salary should permit him and his wife and child to live decently, without undue anxiety, and without the constant pressure to pick up dollars in nonuniversity activities. And if it be said that colleges cannot afford to do this, then I say that American higher education is in a parlous situation; it is displaying at the masthead the banner of high ideals but is really a sort of academic sweatshop.

All the various stages of academic rank should be proportionately compensated. A full professor should receive no less than $8,000 per annum on the basis of the present cost of living; that certainly is not too much when compared with the earnings of successful physicians and lawyers. And assuredly the college professor deserves at least as high a reward from society as they do.

It may be argued that since colleges and universities nowadays secure instructors in spite of paying them low salaries, society need not worry about increasing these. But we may be sure that young men trying to determine whether they should enter a university career will not be encouraged to do so by present conditions, and the ablest of them may well prefer to enter law or medicine or some other profession which also calls for the use of the mind and at the same time is more remunerative. Besides, if investigation and teaching are of high importance to mankind, should society not realize that worry about finances and the necessity of doing various outside jobs to eke out the family budget seriously curtail the professor's accomplishments in research and effectivenes as a teacher? Then too, his enthusiasm for his work is inevitably dampened by the ever-present anxiety over money.

In all colleges there is, as it were, a period of probation for members of the faculty. Instructors and assistant professors do not have permanent tenure, as associate professors and full professors do. And this is proper. A period of testing is thoroughly justified in reference to a young man in the early stages of his career; on the other hand, assured tenure is highly important to a professor, who might otherwise be dropped after years of devoted service, perhaps merely because the college wishes to save a salary. Scholarly work demands freedom from anxiety, and nothing is more necessary for this than assurance of permanent status.

Most reputable institutions limit the total probationary period to seven or eight years at the most. And this is wise. Within that time the college should be able to make up its mind whether the individual is the kind of person it desires as a permanent member of the staff. It is unfair to keep him dangling in uncertainty for ten or fifteen years and then turn him adrift. An institution cannot with any show of justice take the best years of a man's life and then force him by dismissal to seek a place elsewhere with the question constantly arising why, after so many years, his former college released him.

The process of selecting a new member of the teaching staff is of the highest importance. While, of course, the department in which he is to serve should take the initiative and make the nomination, a committee of professors selected in some impartial manner by the faculty itself should be called on to scrutinize the proposal and report on it to the dean and the president.

Too much care cannot possibly be expended on the choice of personnel. Every effort should be made to have an official of good judgment meet the candidate personally. It must be remembered that the person appointed (whatever his rank) will presumably continue on the faculty indefinitely, gradually climbing the academic ladder. It is far easier to be meticulously careful at the time of the original choice than in later years to terminate his connection with the institution. In the latter case, he may not have met all the expectations entertained at the time he was appointed; but faculty members and departmental chairmen and even (though some may not be willing to believe it) administrative officers are human. The man mentioned has doubtless made close personal ties with many in the faculty, he may perhaps have just bought a home, there has been expensive illness in the family, his wife is expecting another child. All such factors operate unconsciously (yes, and often consciously) to cause an institution to retain an instructor even though he has not thoroughly proved his worth. So (I repeat) it is infinitely better to take the utmost possible pains at the time of initial appointment.

When a member of the faculty has attained what is termed "permanent tenure," it is well-nigh impossible to dismiss him. The only causes which are accepted by college faculties are immoral conduct or proved incompetence. The former is, of course, definite, and I suspect that when a faculty member knows that his guilt can easily be established he prefers to resign rather than be exposed to the odium of a trial before colleagues. Incompetence is much more difficult to establish. Of course, a complete mental collapse is easily determined. But it very rarely occurs that a scholar has retrograded and can be proved no longer fit to teach.

This clearly means that promotion to the associate professorship, the first stage of permanent tenure, should be made with the greatest of care; for to retrace one's steps is almost impossible. Here is demanded the utmost certainty on the part of the officials in charge, a rigid sense of justice, both to the individual and no less to the institution, and a firm backbone when the decision is adverse. It must be remembered that if an incompetent person is advanced and therefore retained indefinitely, the many students who will be under his tutelage throughout the years will be betrayed. Kindness to him (if it really be kindness) is assuredly unkindness to them. And the college exists to educate them, and not to give him a soft and undeserved berth. However, despite all that may be said to the contrary, our college faculties are composed, for the largest part, of earnest, devoted men and women who believe in the work that they are doing and are anxious to make it as effective as possible.

In some colleges (I am, of course, not alluding to colleges exclusively for women, though, curiously enough, some of the remarks I am making here apply in such colleges too) there are a number of women teaching in the various academic grades. Too often they are confined to what are regarded as feminine fields, such as home economics or departmental assignments coupled with the deanship of women. I feel

66

strongly that there is an antifeminist prejudice in many departments and in many institutions. For this there is really no excuse. If women meet the standards that have been set up, they should be treated as men are, and should be given the same academic status. They should not be appointed on inferior attainments, nor on the other hand should more be asked of them than of men. I have seen women on college faculties who measured fully up to the standards of the institution and for whom no apology on the basis of sex needed to be made.

Moreover, a university in the truest sense of the term must not set up qualifications based on nationality, creed, or color. If a German is the best man for the post, appoint him. So too if he is a Pole, a Czech, a Frenchman, an Italian. Scholarship is international, if there is anything under the sun that is international, and men of all bloods have made distinguished contributions to knowledge. I should go further and not hesitate to place on the staff a Chinese, a Japanese, a scholar from India or Pakistan; they have great contributions to make in fields of the utmost importance to mankind. I should likewise by all means place upon the faculty any Negro who is able to meet academic requirements.

Religion should, of course, never prove a barrier. Jew or Gentile, Protestant or Catholic—any man or woman who has the knowledge and the required qualities should find a place in a college faculty. How can any institution claim to be worthy of the democracy under which we live if it excludes Jews or Catholics from its staff or rigorously limits their number? There are too few great scholars to make it excusable to deny entrance to the academic fold to those who, while guaranteed freedom of religion by the Constitution, are prevented by racial or religious bars from doing that for which they are supremely fitted. A real university should be in this respect as all-encompassing as the universe.

Scholarship must be democratic—or what can be? And professors of all nationalities, creeds, and colors will inevitably give students a far better training in true democracy than could any lectures stereotyped on purely conventional lines. They will see that Jews, as a group, are not correctly depicted as devoted to money-grubbing, on the one hand, or as raising the banner of Communism, on the other; they will find cultivated, intelligent men whose religion is Jewish as that of most students is Protestant. Hitler seeking to wipe out the Jews—and indeed all who opposed totalitarianism—has done American scholarship a mighty service in sending to our shores scores of men who have made and are making great contributions to knowledge. Of them can it truly be said, "The stone which the builders refused is become the headstone of the corner."

In like manner, students will come to realize that Catholicism has among its adherents brilliant minds and clear-thinking intellects, and, above all, loyal and patriotic sons and daughters. Japanese will be seen to be far more than vegetable-peddlers or laundrymen; they will be revealed as not only learned men, but possessors of an ancient culture and of a courtesy hard to match among those of other complexions. And nothing will go further to break down the prejudice against Negroes than the presence of some on the faculty; they will be gentlemen in every sense of the term, with minds that need ask no concessions of the whites. Such men and women on the staff will give an education to our youth that they sorely lack and that will mean much to our society when they go forth into it.

I have spoken much of the scholarship and teaching skill that should be sought when appointments to the faculty are made. Yet it must not be forgotten that our institutions are American institutions, supposedly training young men and women to live American lives. Hence, while due acount should be taken of what has just been said, nonetheless it is to be hoped that the faculty would in the main consist not of foreigners, but of men and women whose outlook is thoroughly American, in the best, not the narrow, sense of the term. There should, of course, be no preaching of Americanism, but the point of view of Americans of the finest type will inevitably affect the thinking of the young Americans who come under their influence. The line is not an easy one to draw, but there is no doubt that those who are sincerely devoted to this nation will without effort on their part make an imprint on the minds—yes, and the lives too—of their students.

VII.
Departments

Our faculties work together in harmony.

CHARLES FLETCHER DOLE, *The Hope of Immortality*

A DEPARTMENT is in origin a convenient budgetary unit in an institution, such as History or Chemistry. A new department comes into being when a wholly new field of work is introduced, as for example Scandinavian Languages, or, as often occurs, when an existing department has not only become so large as to be unwieldy in numbers, but also, because of the progress of learning, is made up of persons of widely divergent fields or interests, as when Psychology is separated from Philosophy and set up as a distinct department. These statements are, of course, far more applicable to large universities than to small colleges. No doubt, fission of departments as just described has administrative convenience, and may even be necessary, but assuredly it tends more and more to the separation of kindred subjects, or even integral parts of the same subject, and a consequent narrowing of the interests of both students and teachers.

Here a small college has a great advantage; it can place all the social sciences, for example, in one unit. Then there will not be set up sharp lines between History and Political Science, and in departmental meetings a broader point of view will prevail than

70

when the two are separated. Moreover, if any special field has a staff that is rather weak, the association in the same department with stronger members from related fields will prove a great stimulus to the others.

Each of the departments must have a leader or chairman. The notion of a permanent, unchanging departmental head is most unfortunate; for as years go by, he may find it all too convenient to choose the easiest course of action and, when vacancies occur, nominate men who have either been undergraduates in the department or have obtained the doctorate there. In short, inbreeding is likely to occur. Moreover, the initial enthusiasm with which a man enters upon such a headship may gradually disappear, and the department will then move along in a rut, becoming impervious to new ideas, even from new fields in its own area of knowledge.

The chairmanship might well be assigned for a period of years (say five) and the incumbent then be released from its responsibilities. A rotating chairmanship is obviously far more likely to be free from a dictatorial attitude than one that is permanent. It may well encourage sycophancy, too, toward "the chief" if his authority is known to be of indefinite duration. If the chairman knows that his post is but temporary, he will be inclined to consult his colleagues on all important matters and conduct departmental business democratically. This does not mean that when appointments or promotions are to be made he must do whatever a departmental vote or conference decides. The chairmanship is his responsibility, and in such matters he is merely receiving counsel, not instructions; the decision must be his.

It is an advantage to have as chairman a man with a reputation in the scholarly world; obviously, if he writes to a colleague in another institution asking for suggestions concerning personnel or the like, his communication will command a degree of attention which it would not if he were unknown outside the confines of his college. But that is not sufficient. Judgment in the choice of men for the staff must be his, and backbone too to stand by his own decision in these matters, even if there is pressure to bring in or promote some alumnus who is a friend of several members of the department or perhaps, it may be, of some of the trustees. Of course, it is desirable if tact be exercised as well as judgment and firmness.

Too often a chairman is loaded down with a heavy burden of routine work; endless forms must be signed and statistics submitted. It is axiomatic that a scholar should not be expected to spend his time on work of this kind, which ought to be done by a clerk. Incidentally, in departmental committees every effort should be made to bring the younger men early into contact with its business. They will welcome the chance to be regarded as associates of older faculty members, and will feel complimented in being given assignments which their seniors often regard as burdens.

Department meetings at regular intervals are desirable, and the chairman should be extremely careful, when presiding, to play the role of a presiding officer, not of a "boss." It is even more important to have frequent informal social gatherings at which the men can really get to know one another. Smokers or luncheons or dinners are all useful means. In short, an *esprit de corps* should be thus built up. Every effort should be made to pour oil on the machinery of relations that may easily creak and to humanize the formal business contacts of those who already are associated closely in their work. It is in the intimate associations within departments that friction is likeliest to occur, and at times even jealousies to arise.

Conferences or seminars at which there are scholarly discussions of topics within the field of the department are extremely important. Too often a scholar (especially in a small department) feels all alone—isolated, as it were—if he has no one with whom to discuss his problems or to whom to submit a piece of research on which he has been working. A departmental conference would meet this situation, and at the same time stimulate those who may be less inclined to engage in research and inspire them to carry on the scholarly work they have been neglecting.

Efforts should be made to see to it that a department is made up neither of older men nor mainly of youngsters. There should be, as far as is possible, a proper distribution among the various ranks and age groups. If there are too many men in their sixties, it will mean, among other things, that at almost one and the same time a large number of members of the department will retire, many places will unfortunately have to be filled simultaneously, and as a result the continuity of policy of the department may be seriously affected. On the other hand, if the young men are overwhelmingly in the majority, it will mean few replacements, little new blood brought in. Moreover, it may then be difficult to guide the department. And besides, when vacancies occur, it is well to bring in young men; but if they already predominate in number, this will still further destroy the proper balance.

Both in the initial appointment of members of the department and in their retention on the staff the interests of the students should never be forgotten. The thousands of them should be borne in mind who, instead of the stimulating instruction that they might have received under inspiring teachers, may for college generation after generation have to endure the wooden, uninspired teaching of men who should never have been appointed or, in any event, should not have been retained. Colleges were not created as sanctuaries for incompetent teachers, but to afford instruction to young men and women, and it is the duty of those in authority to see that it is the best that can be offered. A college can only be great if it is willing to eliminate poor timber; this it should do early in justice both to the man and to the institution.

VIII.
Choosing Professors

Learning has its value.

LA FONTAINE, *The Use of Knowledge*

OBVIOUSLY, the heart of a college is its faculty. The selection of persons for the staff is the most important function of the officers of the institution. In a small college the president should not surrender this responsibility. In a large institution the duty should devolve in the main upon the dean of the university, or whatever his title may be, vice-president, or provost. To be sure, the chairman of the department or the dean of the school should always do the preliminary winnowing of possible candidates. In the large institution the dean will have to lean heavily on the departmental recommendations thus made to him.

The use of a faculty committee (selected in some manner by the faculty itself) to examine the departmental nomination and submit its recommendation upon it is highly desirable. It provides other points of view than that of the department alone, and at the same time makes members of the faculty more university-minded. They themselves are thereby educated to demanding proper standards, which they in turn may be expected to apply when responsibility devolves upon them to submit nominations. It gives freedom from departmental favoritism, on the one hand, and

75

unfair prejudice, on the other. Such committees will, of course, in general contain members of closely related departments, or men who for some special reason have contact with the subject which the appointee would teach.

It is most unfortunate if an appointment is made without a personal interview. After all, paper records and even publications do not tell all that needs to be known about a man. Recommendations are likely to conceal special weaknesses the applicant may have and merely mention his good points. If he has done satisfactory research but has proved an extremely poor teacher, the person questioned about him is likely to emphasize the former fact and either omit the latter entirely or cover it up by some such statement as, "He is probably an average teacher."

There is, of course, the indefinable quality or group of qualities called "personality." The teacher who has it can set his students all afire with interest in his subject, be it Shakespeare or Homer, anthropology or history, chemistry or astronomy. It is hard to know whether a man has it or not. Again and again one finds a teacher a very different person in the classroom from what he is in ordinary conversation. I have seen a man, jolly and jovial in his usual relationships, become dry as dust in his teaching. The opposite may also be the case. Perhaps the best clue is frank conversation with the man's students; a visit to his classroom is also illuminating, though it does present difficulties.

It must always be remembered that it is not only this or that student who is being influenced by an inspiring teacher; for, as John Erskine says, "The teacher, through his pupils, may influence the future, which is perhaps the part of time which most deserves our attention."[1]

All too often, when a faculty vacancy occurs, those who must fill it will seek men who have made a reputation. But scholars of repute may be well on in years—in the late fifties or even the sixties. Under the usual rules they have consequently but few years of service to contribute to the institution to which they go. Often they are uprooted from a college where they have spent many years and sent their roots down deep. In their few years at the new institution they seldom take root. And far more important is the fact that often their life's work, or at least the most significant part of it, has been done. In other words, they contribute very little to the college to which they go except lend it the luster of their reputation, and even that is not certain, since in the eyes of the learned world their names are associated with the institution with which they have already spent so many years. Moreover, they are likely to demand and command large salaries, and often their appointment becomes a disturbing element in relationships within a department.

I have long felt that the ideal plan is to search among the assistant professors in the field in which a faculty member is being sought; a canvass should be made throughout the country, even in the old and highly revered institutions. Men of that rank have obtained their doctorates at least several years before; one should therefore be able to see whether the doctoral dissertation is the end of their scholarly work or the beginning. What has the man been doing in his first

---

[1] *My Life As a Teacher* (Philadelphia: J. B. Lippincott Co., 1948), p. 13.

teaching years? By that time, too, he should have learned considerable about teaching; and his first floundering efforts should have been succeeded by assurance. What breadth of interest he has should certainly be ascertainable by this time.

If the answers to these questions are enthusiastic, I should at once offer the young man advancement to an associate professorship—even to a professorship, if conditions warrant. He will have been caught in his prime, and the recognition thus given will be the greatest of spurs to him. He will be stimulated to even greater achievement by the early recognition of his ability; and by reason of the higher salary he will be freed from financial anxiety for his family, and thus enabled to devote himself with a single mind to his teaching and research. Nothing is more important for an institution than to bring in brilliant young men and give them all possible encouragement. I have always admired the manner in which President Foster chose the early faculty of Reed College and set thereby a high standard for the institution. His small faculty included Dr. Karl T. Compton (later in life President of the Massachusetts Institute of Technology), William F. Ogburn (subsequently Professor of Sociology at the University of Chicago), and the present Senator from Illinois, Paul Douglas (formerly Professor of Economics at the University of Chicago); at the time of their appointment, Compton was twenty-six years old, Ogburn twenty-six, and Douglas twenty-five.

Promotion and pay, I hasten to add, should by no means be the rewards of new men only. They should go no less to men already on the staff. Let those who have the divine spark be sought out and afforded every opportunity and incentive to make the most of their talents. The "lockstep" system of promotion should not dominate. Advancement should be wholly on the basis of ability, not the number of years of service at a particular rank. Unfortunately, there is great danger that attention may get fixed on appointments to the faculty from without. A scholar never seems greater than when you are striving to induce him to come to you, or, on the other hand, when there is danger of his accepting a call elsewhere. But this may be most unfair to the men you have.

It is the professor, the scholar advancing human knowledge and imparting it successfully, who deserves the respect of society. I recall that when I was a student at the University of Berlin in 1913, the bookstores near by were selling postcard photographs of eminent members of the faculty. Such men as Eduard Meyer and Ulrich von Wilamowitz-Möllendorf were among those thus portrayed, and students bought the cards as souvenirs of their great teachers. Such a practice in our colleges would be at least some indication of respect and affection for those who teach; how infinitely more valuable that would be than the collecting of photographs of athletic coaches or athletic heroes, those transitory beings whose glory hangs by the slender thread of victory! Think what they are honored for— a toe accurately placed against a football, a completed throw of the ball to a fellow player, an unobstructed run down the field—and compare this with the lifelong devotion to the true aims of a university manifested by the members of its faculty.

IX.
Obligations of the College to the Faculty

SECURING THE PROFESSOR'S BEST

Behold how good and how pleasant it is for brethren to dwell together in unity.

Psalm 133

SINCE the college relies on its faculty to perform its work and is only successful in accomplishing its aims by virtue of what its faculty members do, it is of the highest importance that they be encouraged to do their best. How can this be brought about?

We start with the assumption that the faculty members have been selected with care. What then? First and foremost there must be cultivated in the academic body an *esprit de corps,* a devotion to the institution and its well-being. Backbiting and envy should, as far as is humanly possible, be eliminated. There should be a pulling together, a feeling of comradeship. And between faculty and administration there should be mutual confidence and trust. The feeling that the word of the president cannot be relied on is one of the most harmful influences from which a college can suffer. The president should take pride in the achievements of his faculty and see to it not only that the individual is congratulated, but also that the entire faculty is apprised of his accomplishments and the delight of the institution in whatever recognition has come to him.

Salaries should be adequate. No teacher, not even the lowest-ranking instructor, should have to seek outside sources of financial support by means of lectures, the writing of textbooks, or other such devices, or live in a state of constant worry over meeting his bills or thinking what in the world would happen if one of the family should fall ill and require a major operation or prolonged hospitalization.

Salaries, I repeat, must be adequate. Is it not fair to say that, instead of raising tuition fees sufficiently to make up the necessary sum, private colleges today are letting the additional cost of education come out of teachers' compensations? I do not say that fees should be raised; but it is ghastly indeed to think that more and more teachers are falling behind in the effort to live within their salaries. Public institutions are often, in effect, making teachers pay what the taxpayers should pay. Either way, the teacher is the sufferer. If this continues, it will become increasingly harder to attract men and women into college teaching, and the quality of the instruction will in turn deteriorate.

In the second place, the teaching load must not be too heavy. If an instructor carries advanced as well as elementary classes, seeks to keep up with the recent literature on the subjects taught, prepares his lectures with care, performs all the incidental duties pertaining to teaching, and carries on his own research in an earnest manner, a program of nine hours of teaching per week, or three classes, is all that he should be expected to handle.

In the third place, there should be precise indications of the ladder of promotion in salary and rank if a teacher meets the standards of the institution. He should be able to pass the test of the probationary period in seven or eight years at most. To keep a man longer than that on a temporary status is manifestly unfair.

The college should have a regulation assuring to any member of the staff on permanent status the right of a trial by a committee of the faculty before he can be dismissed, and the only bases for dismissal should be proved incompetence or moral delinquency. The burden of proof should be on those who seek the dismissal. And the plea that the college made an error in granting permanent tenure should never be accepted as a valid basis for ousting a teacher; the incompetence must be proved to have developed subsequently. The individual should not be penalized and suffer the destruction of his career because the administrative officers of the college later feel that they made a mistake in the first place.

There should be an adequate retirement system. Few places now have one that is really satisfactory. It must be remembered that professors can save little from their salaries, and provision for their old age through a system of joint contributions by the college and the individual is just about all they have to rely on. When, however, at the time of retirement the annuity is purchased (as it properly should be) so as to cover the lives of both husband and wife, it often sinks to a shockingly low level, indeed not as much as a humble clerk in the college receives, and often far less than the young man with the rank of instructor is paid at the beginning of his academic career. And this situation has of course become greatly aggravated by the decline in the purchasing power of the dollar, a slump clearly continuing and one which I doubt many universities or colleges have taken adequate steps to meet. Men and women who are facing retirement are facing a hard time. And those who have already retired have no protection against the steady decrease in the value of the pensions they receive. Years before, when they made their financial plans looking to retirement, conditions were vastly different from those of today, and now they find themselves with real incomes far smaller than those they had every right to anticipate. If the purpose of pensions is what it is asserted to be, namely, to permit those who have given their lives to an institution to live a dignified and secure old age in retirement, then it seems to me that there is an obligation to aid the emeriti by supplementing their present pensions, and at the same time to make proper plans for the retirement of those now in active status. But the subject of retiring allowances is so important that chapter xii has been given over to examination of the entire matter as a question of the first magnitude.

Further considerations under the general heading of the obligations of the college to the faculty are these, stated categorically:

a) There must be provision for sabbatical leaves; and these should be generous, encouraging members of the faculty to take advantage of the opportunity, and not so niggardly that the young professor making use of a leave places a millstone of debt around his neck for years to come.

b) The college must encourage research not only by promoting those whose accomplishments warrant it, but also by providing funds so that scholars may travel to attend the meetings of learned societies, and also that needed assistance may be given in the form of clerical or other help, and the means of securing photographic copies of documents, or of important laboratory equipment.

c) As a corollary to this, money should be available to publish the worthy writings of the members of the faculty. There are, of course, learned journals to which short papers may be sent for publication, but many of them are so clogged with manuscripts that at least a year must pass before an accepted paper appears in print. More important still is the fact that if the researches result in a book, it will rarely promise to sell copies enough to repay the publisher. Here the need of a properly financed university press is most evident. If the institution cannot afford to finance adequately a press of its own, it should in any event provide a fund which will assist members of the faculty to secure publication elsewhere.

d) It is highly important that the college should not only have a very good library, but should also be ready and able to procure books needed both for the classes taught and for the research in which the instructor is engaged. After all, a library is in a very real sense the heart of a university. It is the laboratory of teachers in the humanities and the social sciences. The funds allocated for the purchase of books must not be niggardly. A scholar should have every possible help in the way of books that he requires, even as laboratory equipment is supplied to the scientist. Moreover, one of the best tests of an institution is the size and quality of its library.

e) Illness inevitably befalls members of the faculty. If it lasts but a few days or weeks, colleagues will gladly carry the sick man's work, knowing that in turn the same will be done for them in time of need. But sometimes the illness is protracted, lasting six months or a year or more. The college should be humane, granting full salary for the period of illness; after all, the number likely to be ill for so long a time in any college will be comparatively small, and the benefit to the striken individual and his family will spread out and be reflected in a sense of relief in the hearts of all members of the faculty who visualize themselves in the same situation. If it befalls that a man cannot again resume his duties, he should be granted a disability allowance, adjusted on the basis of his length of service in the institution and the salary which he had at the time his active connection with the college was severed.

I have listed these various matters as obligations of the institution to the faculty. Precise information on each of them should be given to every man invited to join the faculty, so that he can make with certainty his decision to accept or reject the offer. They are touch-stones of the kind of life he may expect to lead in the college inviting him. All too often, either no information on such matters is given to the person invited, or it is so vague and unclear that misunderstanding is likely to arise. A statement covering the various points need not be extensive, but it should make crystal-clear what the individual has a right to expect. After all, he is making a decision of paramount importance to himself and his family.

X.
The Professor's Obligations

A sense of duty pursues us ever.
DANIEL WEBSTER, *Argument on Murder of Captain White*

IN THE academic world there is much emphasis on professorial privileges and tenure, and it is wise that this should be so. All too often, in institutions where that emphasis does not exist, we are likely to see a professor dismissed virtually at the whim of the trustees, especially if he is regarded as too liberal—or, at any rate, somewhat liberal: even the delivery of an address before a labor union has aroused suspicions that a teacher is "pink." When a young man is dismissed merely because his opinions are less conservative than is agreeable to the trustees, the situation is bad enough; when the victim is regarded as too old to be taken on the staff of another institution, it is tragic; for both, the stigma of dismissal and its cause, however unjustified, will at least be a serious handicap. In most institutions, fortunately, there is a protection for the professor against unwarranted dismissal, namely, the provision for a hearing before a committee of the faculty chosen by the faculty itself. And always in the background is the American Association of University Professors, which investigates all such cases as are submitted to it and publishes its report of findings, setting forth in detail what its representatives have discovered. The institution, if found guilty of improper action, is placed under censure and a statement to this effect is published in every succeeding number of the *Bulletin* of the Association (*AAUP*). Unquestionably, these careful investigations, and even more the fear of them, have helped to keep colleges in the proper path. Moreover, in many colleges the faculty participates in matters affecting the budget, new appointments, and promotions, and thus constitutes, in effect, a real part of the administration of the institution.

But privileges always involve responsibilities, and the faculty is not always as zealous as it might be in holding its members to their full duty. Meeting assigned classes regularly; keeping office hours as announced, both at the opening of each term and throughout the year; supervising the work of assistants with care; seeing to it that grading is done scrupulously, and that reports are submitted at the times required; always showing readiness to discuss with a student any question or complaint about his grades; returning with helpful comments the papers required from students; preparing class work with care; lecturing both audibly and with every effort to clarify the subject; maintaining a proper attitude in the classroom, free from aloofness on the one hand, and on the other not descending to cheap witticisms to win a laugh—these are responsibilities easy to name. And there are many others; this list is far from inclusive, very far.

Worst and most unfair of all derelictions are two, which deserve at least a paragraph of comment. A professor asks for a year's leave of absence in order to accept an appointment as visiting lecturer in another college, or to serve the government, or for some similar purpose. The leave is granted. At the end of the year, the absentee requests an extension of a year more. The request, let us say, is granted. Then there may be yet another request, and a still further extension. And all this time, the college cannot fill the post permanently; it is forced to seek temporary substitutes. And then it may happen that the professor, at the end of his protracted leave, resigns to accept an appointment elsewhere. In short, the institution has had its hands tied for several years while he is experimenting with another post and, at the same time, fully protecting himself.

Then there is the professor who receives, in the spring, let us say, official notice of reappointment for the next academic year, and formally accepts the reappointment; but subsequently, perhaps in June, sometimes even in the midst of the summer vacation, he receives an attractive offer from another institution, and with a mere "Hope this will not put you out," he resigns, leaving the department to stagger through the next year with any substitute who may be available at that late date.

Performing either of these acts, the professor thinks first of himself and uses the institution as an effective interim life insurance.

What should be his proper course? Since a leave of absence means that the college guarantees him the resumption of his post, in like manner he should feel obliged to return for a least another year of service in recompense for the year's leave. Again, when the college offers a man an appointment and he accepts, the institution is bound by this contract. Even if, after

88

the appointment has been made, it feels it has made a mistake, or learns of a far better man for the post, none-theless it has committed itself and remains true to its obligation. Is it too much to ask professors to feel a like sense of obligation? They, like the college, have signed a contract, and it is their duty to live up to it.

Let me hasten to say that very few college professors would be guilty of this second type of dereliction. And while I fear that more might be guilty of the first, still I believe that here, too, we can almost always count on a sense of obligation to the institution.

In the university world, as in the American world in general, there has arisen a host (perhaps I should say a horde) of societies and associations. They include organizations of specialists in a particular field, as for example the anthropologists, the geologists, the philosophers, the historians. Then come subdivisions of these larger fields, as for example the historians of science. Next come organizations for the teaching of particular subjects, as the Association of Teachers of Spanish, or of Russian. Then we have the academic curricular associations, as the Association of Schools of Law or Schools of Business. There are also the associations dealing with purely administrative matters, as the organizations of Deans of Men, Deans of Women, Registrars, Admission Officers, and the like. Finally, there are the general over-all associations, as for example the Association of American Universities and the Association of American Colleges. Of course, there is also the all-inclusive American Association of University Professors, which deals with academic and administrative matters alike and seeks to maintain the standards and the freedom of the profession. And we must mention, too, the numerous regional or state organizations, be they the Pacific Coast Branch of the American Historical Association or the Mississippi Valley Historical Society or the Wisconsin Academy of Sciences or the Western College Association. Altogether, it is an imposing group of organizations, perhaps the more so when we remember that in many of them the membership is made up of persons, not of institutions, and requires the payment of dues.

Attendance at meetings of scholarly organizations is important, both as a stimulus to the professor attending and as a means of contact with the leaders in his profession. Sometimes it is an excellent method of "scouting" for new material for the faculty. When the professor is to read a learned paper, the college often defrays part of his travel expenses. It seems to me proper that this be done: the college profits both by the recognition accorded to the member of its faculty and by the value he derives from the trip. To be sure, the professor secures kudos thereby, and I see no reason why he should not expect to spend some of his own money on the journey. Yet I think the college should be as generous as possible, in view of the narrow margin on which professors and their families are living.

The scholar, in turn, should seek to present a paper that is really creditable both to himself and to the institution he represents. It should not be merely an excuse for making a trip to visit a friend or relative or even to examine a library. And whatever information can be gained that is likely to be useful to the college should be transmitted systematically to the proper officials on his return.

I am not so sure of the value of administrative conferences, such as those attended by deans of men. They are, of course, a device by which these officials meet their opposite numbers in other colleges. Yet anything really significant in this field it should be possible to put into print, to be considered at leisure. Indeed, I believe that articles on administrative topics are likely to be more thoughtful and more attentively considered than the papers read at such gatherings. In any event, we have far too many of these organizations, and ought to prune them. After all, it is now five hundred years since Gutenberg began printing, time enough for its utility to be taken into account. Of course, it is gravely questionable whether all the papers that are read at meetings deserve printing, though some of them are unquestionably useful.

Not infrequently at meetings of national associations in Pharmacy, Social Welfare, Physical Education, and the like, the curricula of these subjects are discussed; more than that, a particular curriculum may be set up and made mandatory, and institutions that do not precisely meet the requirements will be removed from the accredited list of the association. This is often a serious matter, since it is on the basis of accredited lists that opportunity to pursue the profession or vocation is determined. All too often the criteria employed are merely quantitative. The number of books in the library, the number of units in specific courses, the number of faculty members holding this or that degree—these are characteristic of the standards applied. It is not quality, but quantity, that is the test. The situation is a dangerous one; it means that each college or university is no longer the master of its own curricula. Were the trustees of a college to set up curricula for the institution, the faculty would protest violently. But these national associations, in which the college has at most only one representative, set up standards which at times run afoul of the general requirements of the institution. Besides, the association includes weak colleges as well as strong, and often the weak are the majority. Most important of all is the fact that a group of specialists from various parts of the country takes out of the hands of any one academic senate the rights which belong to it. It is the duty of all professors to defeat this dangerous practice, which removes from the faculty of an institution the right to determine the curricula under its jurisdiction. No faculty member representing a college at a national association meeting should feel that he is authorized to drop the noose around the neck of his institution.

In fact, this entire practice of accreditation has gone altogether too far. True, it demonstrated its value in ridding the country of medical colleges that were weak and unable to train men adequately for the medical profession. But today, accreditation is so widespread that it involves the setting up of arbitrary criteria and costs large sums of money. In the university world, experimentation should be encouraged, not barred by rigid rules. Besides, does it not seem absurd when professors from weak institutions are designated as examiners and visit some of the great universities of the country to pass upon the accreditation of this or that phase of the institution's work? Worst of all, as I have already indicated, is the fact that state boards rely upon accreditation lists when they pass upon credentials submitted by individuals.

When representatives are sent to meetings of professional associations, for example those of Business Administration, Architecture, or Social Welfare, the university is expected to pay all the expenses of its delegate. Obviously, this is a great encouragement to the creation of associations. And the professor has a trip at the expense of the university. Undoubtedly, there is value in meeting with confreres at other places and discussing common problems with them. The harm comes when the association, in which one's own institution has in all probability but a single representative, sets up rigid curricula and makes them the requirements for accreditation. All too often, the representative plays a part in establishing them although the faculty of his institution, as a whole, has had no opportunity even to consider them. It is a form of academic racket and should be fought. It seems peculiarly improper that the college should have paid to send the professor to the conference and that he should then join others in placing a pistol at the head of his own college.

I remember vividly when the College of Pharmacy of the University of California had two curricula, one two years in length, the other four, on the theory that for many prospective clerks in pharmacies two years' preparation should be sufficient. But entrance to the College was on the same basis as entrance to the University. The national association set up four-year curricula as the only ones which would be approved for accreditation; and so the College was removed from the accredited list, although other colleges with lower academic standards appeared upon it, having accepted the dictum of the association. Later the College too yielded, since accreditation was necessary if its graduates were to be certificated.

What we actually need in the American college and university world is more experimentation, not less, and national organizations too often stifle experimentation. If there must be accreditation, let it be that of the institution as a whole, not of each segment within it. It would not be improper to demand that the setting up of curricula as a requirement for accreditation in special fields be abandoned. And I think that each institution valuing its own integrity should say plainly that unless the interference with curricula ceases, it will withdraw from the national association. Once the leading universities do this, the association will be forced to come to terms.

Such organizations as the American Association of Universities, though its general policy is opposed to the adoption of legislation, should take a stand in this matter. Certainly the universities and colleges of acknowledged repute should be trusted, without regimentation, to watch carefully in each field and set up curricula designed to train their students effectively. Who would not be willing to accept a graduate of the Harvard or the Johns Hopkins Medical School without carefully measuring the number of hours spent on each subject in the curriculum? Let us get away from this standardization, based, as it is, on what is least important in education, namely, that which can be weighed and counted, not on the intrinsic quality of the work.

In regimented curricula there is also a tendency to introduce subject requirements which are unrelated to training for the profession but which appeal to individual members of the committee setting them up, the justification advanced being their importance in giving breadth of culture to students. But surely such requirements should be set up by the college or university, not the professional school. If English is necessary for the future physician, it is no less so for the engineer, the lawyer, or the teacher. But medical colleges should not demand it for admission; it is in no sense essential or prerequisite to the courses in the medical school. If it is regarded as essential for an educated man or woman, let the university or the college of liberal arts impose the requirement.

As will be noted by the examples cited, the curricula set up as necessary for accreditation include, also, prerequisites for admission to them, and here they not only enter into the territory of the college or university, but at times make such numerous demands as to interfere seriously with the meeting of ordinary requirements in the undergraduate college. Almost always, they take away much of the freedom of choice to which the undergraduate is entitled. Only if the subject is really essential to the work of the professional school is it proper to demand a mastery of it as an entrance requirement. But whatever cannot be so justified should be rigidly omitted.

In this important question of curricula required for accreditation of an institution the duty of members of the faculty is clear. They should zealously defend the freedom of the colleges in setting up all curricula and insist that the institutions be released from these shackles and judged wholly by the quality of their work.

XI.
Sabbaticals

A CHANCE TO ADVANCE KNOWLEDGE

Let knowledge grow from more to more.

TENNYSON, *In Memoriam*

S OME institutions of higher learning have a system of
so-called sabbatical leaves.[1] This, as the name implies, means granting the professor the opportunity of
a year's leave of absence at the end of every six years
of active service. The financial provision varies greatly;
sometimes the professor receives for the year of absence half of his annual salary; it is seldom that he
receives more than two-thirds.

It may be asked why there is need of a year's absence. The purpose is, of course, to permit him to carry
on research or investigation. The man on the street may
ask, "But why should he not do this within the regular
academic year?" The inquirer fails to realize that
while, on paper, the professor's teaching schedule appears light, an infinite number of responsibilities accompany it which require many additional hours of his
time. There is the time necessary to prepare for class
work, and particularly for lectures. Reading lists must
be prepared. Teaching assistants must be called into
conference and given instructions. Time must be al-

---

[1] Of the land-grant institutions, about 55 per cent grant sabbatical
leave in some form. Edith Ruebsam, "Sabbatical Leave in Land-
Grant Institutions," *AAUP Bulletin,* Vol. 33 (1947), pp. 717–720.

lotted for student consultations. There are departmental meetings, departmental committee meetings,
faculty meetings, academic senate meetings, senate
committee meetings. There are meetings of special
promotion committees. There are meetings on archi-
tectural plans for new buildings. There are hours spent
on masters' theses and on doctoral dissertations; there
are examinations for masters' candidates and doctoral
candidates. There is the advising of students on their
programs of study—new students, upper-division students, and graduate students. And these activities do
not by any means cover the entire list. Hence the instructor's time for research is decidedly limited. Moreover, his thoughts are so distracted by this myriad of
matters that it is not easy for him to concentrate on his
own study. Besides, these things are pressing; engagements must be kept, whereas research by its very
nature has no stipulated time. For these reasons sabbatical leave is highly important.

On leave, the professor will often find it necessary to
cross the continent or even go to Europe. Besides, it is
important for him to confer with colleagues working
in the same specialized field. He may need to go far for
essential documents or books, or for laboratory mate-
rials and equipment. And, above all, the sabbatical
gives blessed relief from all other university duties and
responsibilities and allows the man to devote himself
completely to investigations in his special field. In that
atmosphere infinitely more can be accomplished than
in hectic days filled with classes, conferences, committee meetings, and the like.

I can vouch personally for the fact that one can
accomplish far more in research while on sabbatical

leave than when absorbed in the round of regular university duties. It is not merely a matter of time (though that is important), but of the opportunity to concentrate on a particular problem without interruption. Conference, too, with scholars working in the same field is most stimulating. The public, I fear, does not always realize that research is an essential part of a university's functions and that sabbatical leave is an extremely important means of forwarding it.

But there is a fly, and it is a very large one, in the ointment. It is the fact that sabbatical leave does not carry full salary. Since the professor can usually save but little after paying his ordinary domestic expenses, it is not easy for him to face a salary reduced by a third or (more often) by a half. If he must travel to some other institution or perhaps to Europe to carry on his work, the financial burden becomes indeed a heavy one. As a result, but a small number of men in any faculty take the year off; they simply can't afford it.

To meet this situation, various other plans have been tried. One plan offers the alternative of a semester (half of the academic year) on full salary or the year on fractional salary. Since a summer vacation of three months precedes or follows the semester, a period of approximately nine months on full salary is thus made available. Another plan is an arrangement by which a leave for a semester on fractional pay (one-half or two-thirds) is granted at the end of a three years' period of teaching.

Some years ago I proposed a plan, which has been put into effect at the University of California, called the "sabbatical in residence." It is only feasible if the teacher finds it possible to do virtually all his research at the institution in which he teaches. Since regular sabbatical leave at the University of California is on the basis of two-thirds of the professor's salary, this plan requires him to teach one class that is regarded as indispensable for the work of the department, at the same time releasing him from all other teaching assignments and from all administrative and committee duties. Accordingly, it grants him full salary and gives him, for research, all his time save that involved in teaching a single class. When this scheme was proposed, doubts were expressed that more than a few members of the faculty would choose it in preference to the other alternatives; it was thought that the professor would want complete release from university duties. However, the event has proved otherwise. The professor is willing to accept the two limitations inherent in the plan, namely, that during the academic year he must carry on his research on his home campus and that he must teach one course. If it becomes necessary for him to visit another library in this country, or even abroad, the summer vacation is available for that purpose; but of course, the plan does not permit the leisurely trip about Europe that has so often marked a professor's sabbatical abroad. The "sabbatical in residence" exists in the University side by side with the other plans, and the professor may choose any one of these when he is eligible for leave.

I regard the sabbatical leave as essential, and personally would favor granting it on full salary. If the financial strain of establishing it on the basis of the completion of six years of teaching be too great for an institution, I should prefer to see it placed at the end of ten years, say; but let the professor have his entire salary and not be in constant anxiety over meeting expenses or (as more often happens) plunge into a debt that cannot be cleared for years. In short, it would be decidedly worth while to experiment with a semester's leave at the end of five years and a year's leave at the end of ten, but, either way, with full salary. If it be urged that ten years is too long an interval between sabbaticals of a full year, I should reply that probably very few men indeed, in the course of their university careers, have taken as many sabbaticals as the decades they have taught. And the provision of full salary would certainly serve as a strong incentive.

The question arises, To what academic rank should leave apply? There are institutions which count toward the sabbatical only the period from the man's entry into the assistant professorship. I agree that men on annual appointment, as instructors usually are, should not be granted sabbatical leave. On the other hand, I feel with equal conviction that the years served as instructor should be counted toward the period required, since everything possible should be done to enable young men to carry on their research and bring it to a conclusion; they should be spurred on. This really means that the instructor loses no chance to take advantage of the leave, since by the time he is eligible for it he should either have attained the assistant professorship or have gone to another institution. By that time his teaching should have passed the experimental stage and he should have buckled down to some problem of research in his own field.

Quite a number of institutions, presumably feeling themselves financially unable to do so, do not grant sabbaticals automatically at the end of a stipulated number of years; they pass not only upon the ability of the college to spare the man from the teaching staff, but also upon the nature of the research he is preparing to carry on, his own qualifications in the field of research, and the number of sabbatical leaves which the institution feels it can grant for any one year.

Two stipulations should, I think, accompany all sabbaticals. In the first place, the applicant should submit a statement of the work he proposes to do and at the end of the leave make a report on the work done. This does not seem to me unreasonable. If the institution makes it possible for the professor to be free from all duties and yet receive a salary, he has a clear obligation to make good use of that time, and the college has a right to know what he accomplishes while on leave. In the second place, the professor should clearly understand that the sabbatical is not a reward which he has fully earned and which carries no obligation to the institution. He should be informed that at the close of his leave he is bound to return to the college, certainly for not less than a year.

Finally, aside from the scholarly work which a year's leave may make possible, the sabbatical brings relief from day-by-day tasks and the professor returns refreshed and exhilarated to his duties. His new vigor is a return gained from the sabbatical which is too often little understood by the public.

XII.
Retirement and Pensions

WHEN THE PROFESSOR GROWS OLD

When the tired player shuffles off the buskin.

OLIVER WENDELL HOLMES, *How Not to Settle It*

IT IS common knowledge that the salaries of professors are low, and that they receive compensations far inferior to those which many men of equal capacity receive in other fields, be they business or professional. Few of even the most eminent college professors receive salaries of $12,000 per year, no matter what contributions they have made to human knowledge. Remember that in 1948–49 the median of maximum salaries for all full professors was $5,893 and the median of minimum salaries was $4,764.[1]

To be sure, college authorities have been worried by the steady increase in the cost of living, and have raised salaries "to the best of their ability." But still the pay is low; the increase has by no means matched the increase in the cost of living. This makes support of a family extremely difficult. After all, in a professor's family the standards of living include, or should include, not only adequate housing, food, and clothing, but frequent attendance at concerts and plays and a library teeming with good books. The children will

---

[1] Henry G. Badger, in the *AAUP Bulletin*, Vol. 34 (1948), pp. 412–413. The comparable figures for 1949–50 would apparently be $6,000 and $5,000, respectively (cf. *AAUP Bulletin*, Vol. 35, 1949, pp. 719–733).

naturally and properly look forward to attending college or university, and will often have to be helped through graduate school or professional school.

We have, then, low salaries and at the same time standards of living that are high in cultural content. Often, too, when the young instructor begins his career, he is carrying a debt for money which enabled him to complete his studies for his doctoral degree. The salary must not only support the family; it must also pay off the debt. All this means that under normal conditions the professor cannot carry much insurance or set aside any considerable sum to help support him and his wife in their old age. He should not speculate in stocks, for he usually lacks the knowledge or the knack to speculate successfully, and he simply cannot afford losses from whatever sum he may toilfully accumulate.

But this picture is a rosy one. It leaves out of account the inevitable illnesses, often expensive illnesses, within every family. It omits the expenditure involved in sabbatical leaves, which includes not only the amount of reduction in the annual salary but also the cost of travel. It is therefore a fact that few—very few—professors with families can do much more than buy a house during their period of active service.

Aside from what the individual can personally accumulate, many colleges have a retirement system for their faculty members which annually deducts from 5 to 7 per cent of a professor's salary, to be matched by an equal amount from the funds of the college; and this total sum is invested so that interest may be added to it. Accordingly, from an instructor's salary of say $3,000 per year there is deducted annually toward the retirement fund a sum between $150 and $210. Obviously this so curtails his salary that it is well-nigh impossible for him to make any further savings whatever. Although it appears generous of colleges to set aside the large sum required to match the contributions of their entire faculties, the money may properly be regarded as an earned part of their salaries, withheld and invested to provide for the day of their retirement.

The age of retirement differs among the institutions: sixty-five is probably the commonest age; some set it at sixty-seven, others at sixty-eight, and still others at seventy. Obviously, the lower the age of retirement, the smaller the annuity which can be purchased from the sum accumulated.

No scientific study has ever been made, and I do not see how any can be made, which can determine the proper age for retirement. Men differ in retention of their mental as of their physical vigor. It depends, too, on the nature of the teaching the professor has to do— whether he has the burden of lecturing to a class of hundreds or conducts small seminars. Does he work with books, or in a laboratory? Does his specialty require field trips, which are the usual thing for geologists, paleontologists, and anthropologists? Does he carry heavy university or departmental administrative burdens? All these factors enter in; it may be (who knows?) that the age of sixty-seven or sixty-eight hits the mean as well as any other. And yet, I have seen men suddenly lose interest in life when their retirement came. Teaching and the other phases of university activity have become so completely a part of their very being that the severance of these ties at times contributes to death soon after retirement. To be sure, a scholar should have research projects which he has longed to complete but from which he has been kept for lack of time, and many men at that period do fling themselves into research and publication, to their own greater happiness. Unfortunately, however, many professors have no "extracurricular" activities which involve contacts with other people. They do not belong to clubs or associations concerned with public affairs; their only organizations are those of their own fields of study, and these usually meet but annually and in various part of the country. I believe that what they miss most sorely is the human contact which retirement removes in taking them from teaching. Research day after day in one's own study, with no students to guide and inspire, may well become dull and tedious for men whose lives have been spent in teaching as well as in research.

During World War II, that section of the History Department at the University of California which deals with Latin America lost all its members at one and the same time: one man was in Chile on governmental service, a second had died, a third had a stroke. There seemed nothing to do but to recall to teaching an eminent scholar who had been retired a few years before. The Regents approved the exception, and I called the professor into my office to discuss arrangements. Finally I said, "Now we shall have to take up the matter of remuneration." He at once replied, "If you don't give me a nickel for the work, I shall be glad to do it."

Is there an answer to the problem? I think there is. The professor at sixty-seven or sixty-eight is, of course, not one who should usually have the burden of lecturing to large classes. He should not have a heavy teaching program. But in his own field, if he is the kind of professor we esteem, he is a master. He knows more in his own area of specialization than any young man can begin to know; its literature is to a large degree at his fingertips.

Why not, then, let the professor at that age give up all his university duties, all his university teaching, save the conduct of an advanced course in his own specialized field? His unique knowledge would be made use of; his research, for which he would have abundant time, would feed into the course. He would have the human contacts that the retired professor of today misses. He would feel himself a real member of the faculty, as indeed he would be, and not that wholly nominal member, a professor emeritus. These older men thus retained should, however, not only be relieved of all university responsibilities, but should also cease to be voting members of their departments; this is essential in order that the guidance of departments may be wholly in the hands of full-time members of the staff.

For the extra service the retained professor might well receive a salary proportionate to his regular salary when he was a full-time member of the faculty, to which would be added, of course, the annuity which would be purchased for him at the age of sixty-seven or sixty-eight. The supplement to his means of support would be of real importance, for college professors' pensions are today disgracefully small. I feel sure that very few receive $3,000 per annum as personal pensions. And since, of course, the professor wishes to provide for the wife who may possibly survive him, he seeks to secure a pension that will continue throughout both their lives. This reduces the sum received, and nowadays seldom leaves the aged professor and his wife as much as $2,100 on which to live. This sum is stated on the assumption that husband and wife are the same age. How far will that go in these times?

And yet, to be realistic, I am aware that it is unreasonable to withdraw more than 7 per cent from a professor's salary toward the retirement fund; and although salary increases are undoubtedly necessary, I doubt very much whether those that may be made will of themselves adequately increase the annuities received.

A large number of the colleges of the country should feel ashamed of the pensions on which their professors are being retired. Even some large and distinguished universities at times retire their emeriti with saccharine words of praise and pensions of $100 per month or a little more. Some eminent scholars have been retired on $50 per month. I admit that these are exceptional cases; nevertheless, how can a university with any self-respect permit its faithful servants to spend their old age in dire poverty? I know of one retired professor who is serving as a night watchman. Without question, there should be a "floor" under all pensions, and none should ever be less than $150 per month; even that is far, far too little.

Those who have recently been retired, or who soon will be, suffer in two ways by inflation. In the first place, their incomes have been severely reduced owing to the drop in interest rates, and in the second place they of course also have to face the great rise in the cost of living. Obviously it is too late for the increase in salaries during recent years to be of material help to them.

Aside from the lessening physical and intellectual vigor imputed to professors who are in their late sixties and seventies, their retirement has been justified by the importance of opening the doors of advancement to younger men. Certainly, older professors who have had the chance to spend their lives in academic posts should not selfishly block the way for the next generation. The plan suggested, however, would turn the leadership of the department over to the younger men and would merely assign a fractional teaching load to the older. The path of advancement would thus be opened up, but without completely eliminating the veterans. It may be argued that this would place a heavier financial burden on the institution; to a limited degree this may be true, but it is certainly the least expensive way to meet the undoubted and justified demand for higher retiring allowances than are today available.

Accordingly, my idea seems to me in the interest of the institution, the advanced students, and not least the professor. It is highly important that the plan apply to all professors reaching the stipulated age (subject always to the professor's own desires), not just a selected few. Otherwise, those not chosen would feel that the institution they had served faithfully for years had struck them a blow; they would regard it as a reflection on their capacity. Besides, if a man has so long been a satisfactory member of the faculty, surely he has not in an instant become so worthless that he is not fit to teach a single course in his own specialty. Moreover, the selection of only a few for retention leaves the annuity needs of the group as a whole unmet.

The men retained should not be called "emeriti," for they will not be retired; their teaching programs will merely be reduced. And that raises the questions: When should they be completely retired? When should they become actually emeriti? When I see judges serving on the bench long past the age of seventy, I wonder whether professors should not continue so to teach as long as life and strength permit.

Professor L. H. Seelye of Robert College has made an interesting and valuable proposal.[2] He suggests the setting up of a Teachers' Continuation Service, an agency by which retired professors could be employed in other institutions either for a brief period as substitutes or for a longer period as regular appointees. But if the professor is prospectively a desirable member for the faculty of another institution, why not continue him at his own, as I have proposed? There the facilities for his work are available, there is his home, and he would continue a real part of his college. The burden imposed on him would not be great, certainly not as great by far as that resting on a judge. In any event, I should favor beginning the plan on that basis; if later it should be deemed necessary to set some arbitrary figure for complete retirement, that can readily be done. But I believe there will be no need to do so; the situation will, I feel, care for itself.

The low pensions which retiring professors now receive have often driven them to seek methods of supplementing their inadequate income. On several

[2] "For the Teacher Aged 65—What?" *AAUP Bulletin,* Vol. 34 (1948), p. 89.

occasions when I was active in administration I was visited by able professors, just retired from their own institutions at the compulsory age of sixty-five, who sought appointments at the University of California for the period yet remaining before they should reach the age of retirement established there. That it was usually necessary to decline their services was a source of deep regret to me, partly because they would have been assets to any institution, and partly because I wished I could help them in their financial difficulty. Some men in their situation have, however, succeeded in obtaining positions as peripatetic instructors for a limited number of years, in universities here and there throughout the country. Others on the retired list are willing to accept almost any kind of work, even far from the field of teaching, to eke out their meager annuities. This is all to their credit; but assuredly it is not to the credit of their colleges.

An interesting experiment has been carried on for some years now, at Hastings College of the Law, an affiliated institution of the University of California, situated in San Francisco. It has deliberately sought professors of distinction who are about to retire from other law schools, and has appointed them on its staff; Harvard, Yale, California, Stanford, and other universities are represented. The group is termed the "Sixty-five Club," and several of its members have passed seventy years of age. The results, I understand, have been excellent. It is the policy of the College to retire these men at the age of seventy-five years. The Dean in a letter speaks not only of "the industry, ability, and experience," but also of "the inspiration and enthusiasm" of the members of the "Club." The plan seems to me a strong argument for the proposal I have made.

The New School for Social Research has recently embarked on the same policy, through the influence of its president emeritus, Alvin Johnson. Ten "retired" professors in a variety of fields, ranging from law to child behavior, from mathematics to general literature, have been placed on the staff. "Johnson hopes that other institutions around the country will follow the New School's example. 'My little project is the edge of the wedge,' says he. 'I mean to put this idea over.' "[3] Certainly, these experiments show how valuable an intellectual resource we have been neglecting.

[3] *Time*, October 2, 1950, p. 60. Quoted by courtesy of *Time*; copyright Time Inc., 1950.

XIII.
The Students

IT EXISTS FOR THEM

Much study is a weariness of the flesh.

Ecclesiastes 12: 12

WHEN ALL is said and done, colleges and universities came into being and continue to live for the sake of students. Undoubtedly, research is of high importance to mankind, but I am convinced that there would be comparatively few institutions of this type, were there no students. Private benefactors and the several states were interested first and foremost in the young men and women who desired to receive an education.

What sort of young people are they? The answer is, of course, "All kinds." There is the solemn "grind" who devotes himself wholly to his assigned college work, his books, his laboratory. There is the very good student who does more than merely meet assignments, who is keenly interested in his college work and reads widely in the fringe material of the subjects of his course, even though he is under no compulsion to do so. There is also the good student who takes an interest in cultural matters outside of his assignments and plays some part in extracurricular activities. There are those who have to work long hours for room and board and tuition fees and whose time is given up wholly to such work and preparation for college classes. Besides, there

112

are those who come to college for social purposes, join the "best" fraternities or sororities, love to "bum" about the house, spend much time "queening" (or whatever term has replaced this for squiring the members of the feminine sex) and at dances and in similar gregarious activities. Some there are (and indeed a considerable number) who give themselves overwhelmingly to extracurricular activities—be they athletics, student-body government, undergraduate politics, journalism, or any of the many other aspects under which these activities appear; these too, like the social set, are apt to slide through with a minimum amount of studying. They, and other groups as well, are aided by coaches and most of all by the so-called "Phi Bete" notes, carefully taken down from the lips of the lecturers by competent reporters in the classrooms and sold for a modest sum to those who have found other matters too important to permit attendance at lectures. There are combinations of these various groups in differing degrees. In fact, there are as many kinds of individuals in college as there are in society as a whole.

I firmly believe there are not enough of the type which we think of as ideal, those who do their required work well but do not consider that their reading on the topic is satisfied when they have gone through the assigned number of pages. They read, moreover, far beyond the call of duty in fields in which they are not taking courses—great works of literature, important histories, philosophical writings, books on modern discoveries in the sciences, and a host of other topics. They take advantage of opportunities to hear concerts, visit art exhibits, and attend lectures on a wide variety of subjects. They join discussion groups on current problems, national and international. They have group contacts with students of differing backgrounds and with foreign students from all segments of the globe. How rare, in both senses of the term, are students like these! And when I think of this, I wonder whether, to some degree at least, the colleges have not been remiss in their duty. In some way there should be aroused such a belief in the value of that for which students presumably come to college, and of the other cultural activities which college provides, that students will seek after these things with avidity, rather than regard them as disagreeable interruptions to the delightful but superficial aspects of college life.

In their discussions and newspaper articles, students show increasing freedom from prejudice where those of other colors, ancestries, and creeds are concerned. They object strenuously when they learn that, in employment, color lines are being drawn. And yet in many ways they themselves draw them, most notably in their fraternities and sororities (which I discuss in a separate chapter). But in the various student-body activities the old prejudices are yet to be seen. How many student-body officials are drawn from what are termed minority groups? How many class officers are foreign-born? How many top positions in student publications are held by members of minorities? We could go up and down the entire list of student activities and find the same situation. Doubtless throughout the land exceptions may be found, but I believe these are not very numerous.

It must in frankness be admitted that these exceptions are today becoming relatively more frequent and positions of esteem in the eyes of the students are being opened to aspirants formerly debarred. When a Negro is chosen Yale's football captain, another serves as president of the Student Council of the Y.M.C.A. at the University of California, and a third is president of the National Student Association, we must concede that real progress has been made. These are highly encouraging signs; but if our college population does not choose on the basis of individual capacity rather than such externals as color, who should?

To be sure, societies such as Phi Beta Kappa draw no prejudicial lines in the institutions known to me; and the same is true of organizations closely allied with the work of departments, such as the Classical Club, the Chemistry Society, and the like. But in these the faculty often plays a considerable part, and outstanding scholarship in the particular field is, of course, too obvious to be slighted in an organization existing to foster discussion in that area of knowledge. But where free choice is made by the students, consciously or unconsciously discrimination frequently rears its ugly head.

Students reside in fraternities, in sororities, in student coöperatives, in college-owned dormitories, in boardinghouses, in apartments, and in homes with their own families. Of all these places of residence by far the most desirable is the college dormitory. First and foremost, like the houses of fraternities and sororities, it enables the student to live with other students, to eat with them, to discuss with them, to play with them. The solitary student is a pathetic figure; almost invariably, he has but the most meager resources. He lives in a room by himself, often prepares his own frugal breakfast, eats one meal—and that a cheap one—at some more than modest restaurant, cafeteria, or "beanery"; if there is a third meal, it may well consist of a cup of coffee and a piece of bread. He can't afford to participate in student activities or go to the theater or to concerts. He lives a most unfortunate life, often a most unhappy one. He lacks human contacts, may easily brood over some fancied injustice, and even decide that life is not worth living. If he survives it all, he will not by any means be equipped for human society; the chances are against his success as teacher, lawyer, or businessman. At the opposite pole the fraternity stresses that which to be sure is a part of college life; but it overstresses it. The social side comes first, and hours are spent loafing on the steps of the fraternity house. Its standards are often false standards. Its selection of members is on an undemocratic basis.

The dormitory furnishes association with other students without making the social aspect of first importance. Its members constitute a cross section of the student body, and no discrimination should ever enter into a college-controlled dormitory. There is no "eternal" tie binding its members, but the group is large enough to permit each member to find kindred spirits and form lasting friendships. It promotes the democratic ideals which should animate the college. It places first things first—scholarship, for one—but does not neglect the social ties which are important to every human being.

The dormitories should not be luxurious; if they are, living in them becomes costly and only students of means can afford to reside in them. Besides, even if it were possible to set the rates fairly low, they would give to a student with modest funds four years of surroundings which would make him critical of his home and set standards for him which in all probability he could not soon or easily attain in later years. But they should, on the other hand, not be barracks and aim at extreme economy; they should not be on the level of bare subsistence. After all, the surroundings amid which one lives cannot help but influence him. They should strike a mean between the luxurious on the one hand and bedrock economy on the other.

At times the question is asked whether it is proper or necessary for a college to have dormitories. Assuredly the college is interested in the whole student, not merely the part of him which sits in the classroom or works at a laboratory table. It must, then, be concerned with his living conditions; he must have adequate food, a proper bedroom, a satisfactory place to study, the necessary heating. More than this, the atmosphere in which he lives should be conducive not only to proper studying, but to making him in as many ways as possible a worthy member of society. Hence I feel that a college is performing a highly important task when it builds and conducts dormitories. After all, it seems illogical to have a well-equipped hospital on the campus, and care for students when illness, even of the slightest, overtakes them, and at the same time to have no concern for the conditions under which they live day by day, conditions which may often affect them physically. Assuredly, a hospital is important: student illnesses are cared for in the incipient stages, thus safeguarding the health not only of those who receive the direct benefit of treatment, but also of those with whom they associate. The parents of students should feel a great sense of reassurance from knowing that in case of illness their children will be well cared for. But illness is the exceptional condition; the manner of student's living is an affair of all the days, day after day.

Wherever possible, it is beneficial if a faculty member or, better still, a faculty member and his wife live in the dormitory, not as monitors, but to be available for counsel and to help guide the students in their activities. For example, a professor might at intervals be invited to join in informal discussion with the students concerning a topic in his own area of knowledge which is to the fore in general interest at the time. Moreover, the faculty counselor could do much, very much, to set the tone of the house.

What chance has a student to enter a professional school within the university? The number of qualified applicants may far exceed the available facilities. This is true for medicine, and has been so for many years. In my youth, students went directly from high school to medical school, and every eligible applicant was admitted; today, but a small fraction of the applicants can be accepted. Engineering has reached this point, dentistry likewise, and business administration is approaching it.

The question of selection at once arises. Various devices are employed. First and most usual is a choice on the basis of the prior academic record of the students applying. In general, particular emphasis rests on the grades in the subjects that are regarded as fundamental to the work of the school or college to be entered; thus for medicine the grades in the spe-

cifically premedical subjects, chemistry, physics, zoölogy, are likely to play a considerable part. In many
fields there are aptitude tests which are used alone
or in combination with grades. Some schools place
much store on personal interviews, usually combined
with grades or aptitude tests or both. Letters of recommendation are often required. Letters should be
scrutinized with great care; obviously the persons
asked to write such letters are chosen by the candidate,
no doubt because they are regarded as friendly. The
writers (such is human nature) will seldom write anything to the candidate's disadvantage; if they know
of defects, they will usually omit mention of them.

Interviews impose a heavy responsibility on the
examiners. The reflection that on the basis of a conversation of say thirty minutes an examiner will decide
the course of the candidate's entire career (by opening
or closing the doors to the profession he seeks to enter)
places a heavy burden on a conscientious man. Moreover, the poor boy, acutely conscious of his shabby
clothes, desperately anxious to gain admission, may
as a result make a worse showing than the son of a
fellow citizen who is accustomed to all types of guests
in his home and feels quite at ease with the examiner.
Besides, human nature being what it is, the son or
daughter of a governor, a prominent banker, or a
fellow practitioner of the profession to which admission is sought will inevitably start with a great bias in
his favor.

Finally, there is the ever-present question of discrimination, be it on the basis of sex, religion, color,
or ancestry. It is well known that many colleges admit
Jews by quotas. Indeed, some admit frankly that they

will admit no Jews, or no Catholics, or no Negroes, or no Chinese, or no Japanese. The foreign-born are very much and very often handicapped. Women are seldom given an even chance in professional schools. "It requires no parade of statistics to know that the situation for young people of minority groups is today unsatisfactory, both in their opportunity to enter college and in the happiness of their college life."[1]

That this is undemocratic is obvious. Worse than that, it unfairly denies to an able boy or girl the chance of developing to the fullest. Most important of all, society is denied the opportunity to profit by the talent and skill of those who have the ability but who find the doors closed because they are black or because they are females. After all, science knows no barriers of this kind; it unlocks its mysteries to those who have the talent, regardless of sex or creed. A Naguchi would probably have found it difficult to gain admission to many of our medical schools. And I believe that when the beloved member of a family lies sorely stricken and death threatens, the family does not care whether the skilled physician is man or woman, Protestant, Catholic, or Jewish, even Negro, Chinese, or Japanese, provided only he will bring relief.

The problem of selecting students for these overcrowded specialties is, I grant, a difficult one, but it must be worked out objectively, without undue influence on the one hand or prejudice on the other. I know it may be argued that society cannot make use

[1] *Higher Education for American Democracy* (Report of President's Commission on Higher Education, December, 1947), Vol. II, p. 25. Harper & Brothers are the publishers.

of a host of Negro physicians. This is a rather grim joke when one realizes how very few medical schools are open to them, and how badly off the Negro population is for medical men. The ratio of physicians to the white population is 1 to 843, but to the black it is but 1 to 4,409; in short, the Negro practitioner must care for five times as many persons as the white physician. In the South the condition is shocking; in South Carolina there is but one Negro physician to each 12,151 of his fellows, and in Mississippi one to every 18,527. What wonder that the mortality rate for Negroes is higher than that for Caucasians?[2] But if (and this is a great "if") the number of Negro physicians should prove at any time to exceed the demand, will not our system of free enterprise take care of that, even as it does when there are too many engineers or too many chemists? No, I fear that this is but a subterfuge, and a very transparent one, masking prejudice. In any event, it is utterly unjust to make estimates of the number of a given group to be trained in a given profession on the basis of the ratio of that group to the total population. It is the ability of the individual alone that should count; that and nothing else. If persons of a certain minority show a particular skill in medicine, for example, society should be glad to avail itself of their ability.

Private institutions have no more right to set up quotas or barriers against the admission of those of minority groups than public institutions. A democratic society cannot tolerate undemocratic practices on the part of either type of college. Freedom from taxation

[2] Glen E. Carlson, "Discrimination in Higher Education," *Western College Association, Proceedings,* April 10, 1948, p. 26.

is one means of public aid to private institutions, the G.I. Bill indirectly has been another; other forms of assistance are not unlikely to be given in the future. But even if not a cent came to them from taxation, they would have no right to prove recreant to the ideals both of democracy and of truth. If laws are regarded as sound which restrain restaurants or hotels from refusing service to anyone because of color, how much more appropriate is the demand that institutions professing to hold aloft the torch of truth must cease to make themselves tools of discrimination and prejudice![3]

Should a student choose a college in his home town, or one at a distance? If he can afford to do so, let him by all means go away from home; he is then no longer the boy still in the bosom of his family, but a college student living with his companions and having the benefit of such associations. When he goes from home, he ought to select either a small college noted for its influence upon its students or a university famed for its scholarship; if the latter, he should try to go to the university strongest in the field of his interest. Assuredly, he should never choose an institution merely because it has a strong football or basketball team or because he knows a fraternity member who assures him that the brothers will give him a "rush."

One's college years will play a very large part in determining his character, his attitude toward the world, and the kind of life he will lead. Let each choose the institution that will do most for him—not

[3] Cf. also *To Secure These Rights* (Report of the President's Committee on Civil Rights; U. S. Government Printing Office, Washington, D.C., 1947), pp. 65 ff.

for the star football player, or the social climber, or even the mere grind, but for himself as a person; the one that will help to make him more nearly the kind of man he aspires to be. If financial conditions make it necessary that he attend the college in his home town, let him remember that what one gets out of college depends far more on the student than the type of institution. Some of our greatest men in all fields—not excluding scholarship—have had their educational training, at least in their earlier years, in colleges by no means of the first rank.

XIV.
Scholarships

SOCIETY NEEDS THE BEST

A scent for "pairts" in his laddies.
IAN MACLAREN, *Beside the Bonnie Briar Bush*

GOING to college has become so common that it is often forgotten how expensive a business it is. First and foremost, if the family is in poor or even modest circumstances, it must face the loss of the wages that John would have earned had he not gone to college. That, however, is only the beginning. There is the tuition fee, often amounting to $500 or $600 per year; for a four-year program we have a total expenditure for fees alone amounting to at least $2,000 and frequently reaching $2,400 or even more. This is a heavy burden for those in modest circumstances, especially in these days when the cost of living is high. To be sure, in the Middle West, South, and West there are state institutions which are supported by the people of the commonwealth through taxation and which offer free tuition. This is a great help, although in few of these institutions are there no fees at all. At both private and state colleges there is another and inescapable expense, namely, for food and shelter and laundry, and also for books and whatever equipment students are expected to own personally. I leave out of consideration clothing and transportation to and from the seat of the university. On a modest but by no means luxurious basis the cost of food, shelter, and so on, has been estimated at $800 per annum. For a four-year period that means an outlay of $3,200. In other words, there is a heavy demand on a student's finances where no tuition fee is imposed.

Because of these burdens it is certain that there are many able young men and women who do not go to college or who do not complete their college course. "More than 9 per cent of the boys and girls in Pennsylvania who were of college caliber but of below-average means ... did not go to college. ... These estimates give reason for saying that out of every hundred young people between six and nine are good college material but do not reach college."[1]

A study was made of 1,023 able students graduated from Milwaukee high schools in 1937 and 1938, all with an intelligence quotient of 117 or above. It is clearly shown that "the higher the parents' income, the greater is the proportion who went to college. Thus where the income is $5,000 or more, 92 per cent of the children will be in college, while where the income is $1,000 to $1,499 the per cent in college is but 25.5."[2] President Conant of Harvard has repeatedly emphasized the fact that our educational system is in reality not democratic since such a throng of able men and women have for financial reasons been denied the opportunity that their talents warranted.

In the brochure entitled *Economy in Higher Education* the following statement appears: "The largest

---

[1] *General Education in a Free Society: Report of the Harvard Committee* (Harvard University Press, 1945), p. 88.

[2] Quoted by William L. Warner, Robert J. Havighurst, and Martin B. Loeb, in *Who Shall Be Educated?* (New York: Harper & Brothers, 1944), pp. 52–53.

item in the average student's expense account is usually living expenses. Even where tuition fees are low or covered by scholarships, the student usually has to raise the money somewhere for his board and room. Of the thousands of students unable to enter college or forced to leave because of finances, this item is in most cases the insurmountable obstacle."[3] On the other hand, the G.I. Bill of Rights has made higher education possible for thousands of men and women who did not dream that they could ever go to college; it is creating for our country a vast number of trained men in a great variety of fields, who under normal conditions would not have had a chance at a college education.

The President's Commission on Higher Education sums it up succinctly: "This Commission concludes that the decision as to who shall go to college is at present influenced far too much by economic considerations. These include inadequacy of family income, the opportunity today afforded young people out of high school to earn relatively high wages, and the increasingly high living costs for students forced to live away from home while in college. These factors combine to keep out of college many who have the abilities which would enable them to profit substantially by a college course of study."[4]

Dr. Hutchins, recently chancellor at Chicago, in commenting on the report said: "[The Commission] is right in pointing out that higher education in the

[3] David S. Hill and Fred J. Kelly, *Economy in Higher Education* (New York: Carnegie Foundation for the Advancement of Teaching, 1933), p. 108.

[4] Vol. II, p. 16.

ILLUSTRATIONS

Hamilton M. Wright photo

THE ROTUNDA, UNIVERSITY OF VIRGINIA

Joe Rosenthal photo

COMMENCEMENT AT STANFORD

Associated Press photo

THE CHAPEL AT PRINCETON

H. Parker Rolfe photo

THE LIBRARY AT BRYN MAWR

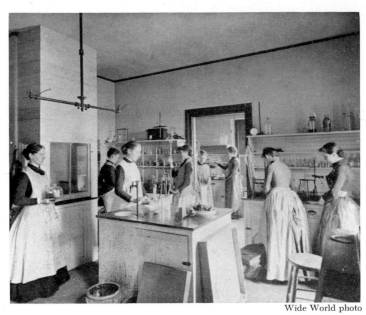

Wide World photo

WELLESLEY: SCIENCE LABORATORY, 1886

Bob Lynds photo

STUDENTS FROM SEVENTEEN COUNTRIES

CANDIDATES FOR HONORARY DEGREES

MEMBERS OF THE "SIXTY-FIVE CLUB"

HARVARD CREWS AT PRACTICE

THE TENSION OF THE "BIG GAME"

Courtesy of the Sun and Times Co.

"AND NOT ONE CENT MORE DO WE PAY YOU MEN!—THIS SCHOOL DOESN'T OVEREMPHASIZE SPORTS!"

GREAT PRESIDENTS OF THE PAST

Wheeler, of California, and Eliot, Harvard; Jordan, of Stanford, and Gilman,
Johns Hopkins; Angell, of Michigan, and Harper, Chicago

Scholarships

United States is free only in the sense that public colleges and universities charge low fees or none. Higher education is not free in the sense that students without money can avail themselves of it. The cost of living and the loss of earning power to their families prevent many young people from going to a free college. They are just as well qualified as those who go. Many of those who go do so because they can afford it. Many of those who do not go don't because they can't. The Commission properly insists that the economic condition of a young person's parents should not determine his educational opportunities. The Commission sees that the economic barriers to educational opportunity must be broken down by the federal government."[5]

It will, of course be pointed out that every college offers scholarships. They do; but even in many of the best institutions the number is pitifully small. Thus Johns Hopkins has 318 undergraduate scholarships, Minnesota 170, Yale 576, and California (Berkeley) 444. Besides, in the main they are virtually grants-in-aid, not real scholarships. Thus at one university the average amount of the annual scholarship is $300, little more than one-third the cost of living on a modest basis. That there are too few scholarships is indicated, moreover, by the fact that at some institutions about three times as many students who are scholastically eligible apply for them as there are scholarships. In some colleges also, freshmen are either debarred from holding scholarships or at least have but slight opportunity to obtain them. Those who award them desire to see the records of the applicants in college for at

[5] *Educational Record,* April, 1948, p. 108.

least a term (preferably a year) before the grants are made. For many a student this locks the door to a college education.

I can at once hear the indignant question: "But why doesn't he work his way through college? Throngs have done it." Personally, I do not think that a small amount of self-help harms a boy or girl; indeed, it is usually advantageous. It gives him a useful contact with the world into which he is going, and the time spent is not so great as to prove injurious. But far too often too much time, too much strength, too much energy are devoted to working one's way through college. The boy who works six or eight hours a day has neither the time nor the mental attitude to profit from his studies. He will skim over his college assignments, dash through them in the few hours the day still holds—and lose the zest for intellectual activities that college should give. Often he will cut short his hours of sleep. In his youth he will feel equal to it, but he will pay for it in later years. Because time presses he will eat improperly and hastily, and for that too a price will some day be exacted.

The young man whose account of his college days is presented by Dean Christian Gauss sets forth his situation clearly: "I was in that continual dilemma of which I spoke—I did not dare neglect my studies for fear of the faculty, and I did not dare neglect my work for fear of the treasurer. . . . While I was doing my work I worried about my lessons, and while I was studying I worried about money."[6]

Besides, college years should not be a period in

[6] *Through College on Nothing a Year* (New York: Charles Scribner's Sons, 1915), pp. 94–95.

which a student spends a minimum of time on his studies; he should be tempted to read more in a subject than the prescribed assignment. And, having available a great college library, he should voluntarily read in fields remote from his courses and browse to his heart's content in history and art and literature. This is his chance not only to be educated, but to educate himself. This is the time to acquire a taste for reading, good reading, which will be a source of great pleasure and broad interest throughout his life. And association with his fellow students is assuredly an educational experience of value. But for the student working his way these things are reduced to a minimum, or may even be nonexistent.

Working one's way through college is regarded as praiseworthy by those who in their hearts place it ahead of the work of the university. To them, getting through somehow and securing that accolade, the bachelor's degree, is all-important. The late T. R. Glover, the distinguished English classical scholar, told me that once he had attended a dinner at one of our American universities. An official, I think it was the president, boasted in his address of the number of students who had worked their way through college. The Englishman said he had been tempted to leap upon the table and shout, "Shame on you for thus wasting the talents of your able young men!" The point is, I think, thoroughly valid. If these men and women are worth educating, and their education is really worth while, it should be their major activity, and should stimulate them to do far more than skim through assigned pages or dash off assigned papers. Their minds should be inspired to self-activity, and only freedom of time can even begin to make this possible.

Thomas Jefferson saw the need clearly when he proposed his educational program for Virginia: "In order 'to avail the commonwealth of those talents and virtues which nature has sown as liberally among the poor as among the rich, and which are lost to their country by the want of means of their cultivation,' the visitors would select every year a certain number of promising scholars from the ward schools to be sent to the colleges and from the colleges to be sent to the university at the public expense."[7]

In many institutions there is far more money in the Loan Fund than is available annually in the form of scholarships. The generous donors think it is better to lend a student a sum of money which he must in time repay than give it to him outright in the form of a scholarship. Incidentally, it should be pointed out that not infrequently a student who has had an undergraduate scholarship later returns to the college the sum he has received, to be used as a scholarship for another student. But let us ask ourselves what the purpose of a scholarship is. It aims to make it possible for a needy student of greater than average ability to secure an education and thereby render greater service to society than he could give if he were denied the chance to go to college. In short, every such student, if properly selected, is a potential source of great usefulness to his fellow men. If a scholarship makes it possible for a young man or woman to go through college and become a great physician, a great teacher, a

---

[7] Gilbert Chinard, *Thomas Jefferson, the Apostle of Americanism* (Boston: Little, Brown & Co., 1944), p. 508.

great public official, should we not be satisfied? Is this not far better than to dole out a few dollars as a loan and keep the student in constant anxiety over the repayment? One who receives a scholarship makes a far greater return in the kind of life he lives and the professional service he renders. Loans are useful for unanticipated emergencies, as devices to help students when books are stolen or illness at home calls for a journey; but they should never be regarded as substitutes for scholarships.

We should have in all our colleges a large number of scholarships, many more than at present, and they should be great enough in amount to care for the student's subsistence and books if the institution is publicly supported, and in addition his tuition fees if it is a private college. The awards should be made with the utmost care, and, though the financial condition of the applicant must be taken into account, should place by far the greatest emphasis on ability, intellectual power, and, as far as can be gauged, promise. This means that the committee in charge should have ample assistance, and time for investigating each case most carefully. School records, intelligence tests, personal interviews—all should be employed. Letters of recommendation should be asked for, even though, as has already been pointed out, these often have to be read with great discrimination. It has already been emphasized that care should be exercised in interviews. It would be distinctly worth while to experiment with the awarding of scholarships on a basis of competitive examinations; certainly a competitive system would make it possible to grant them on a purely objective basis.

In the same way we need many, many more graduate fellowships, adequate in amount. After all, if the undergraduate should have ample time to devote himself to intellectual pursuits, it is even more necessary that the graduate student should be able to spend all his time on his studies and other activities that concern an educated man. Certainly no medical or legal student should for a moment be permitted to work his way through the professional school; indeed, if the school is worthy of its name, it can't be done. The professional studies themselves consume practically all the student's time; what little is left, and assuredly it is little, should be spent both in reading current history and in discovering something of the great works of literature, history, and the like, in going to concerts, to the opera, to art exhibitions, to worthwhile plays. The world is so full of a number of things that one wishes he had the leisure theoretically open to kings.

But the graduate student in other fields, such as chemistry or anthropology, history or English, is in a similar situation. There are countless works in his own field which he ought to read, quite aside from the class assignments, seminars, theses, dissertation requirements. And he too should be encouraged to make himself a broadly educated, cultivated man.

It must not be forgotten, also, that nowadays an increasingly large number of graduate students are married. Some of my readers may shake their heads and say: "They ought not to be married. And there is no reason why this fact should enter into the award of fellowships." But their marriage is a fact, and one which can hardly be altered save by divorce—which

132

the college will scarcely demand. If the young man is extremely able, it is not only to his advantage but to that of society as well that he be encouraged and helped toward the completion of his studies. Brilliant men and women in any field are not so numerous that any should be denied the opportunity they seek, merely because they followed a human impulse and got married.

Graduate fellowships, then, should not only be as large as undergraduate scholarships, but considerably larger, so that without worry or anxiety the potential lawyers, physicians, architects, engineers, public-health officers, professors in every field from anatomy to zoölogy, may be able to develop to their fullest. Of course, they will not expect to be supported in luxury, but will be grateful for decent surroundings and adequate food for themselves and their wives and children.

It is always to be remembered that it is society that profits when able men and women who come from the lower economic strata are encouraged so to train themselves as to make them valuable servants of mankind in a myriad of fields. The student is a gainer by his education, of course, but far more does society gain, whose sick he heals, whose innocent he defends, whose industries he aids by new devices, whose homes he plans, whose youth he teaches in many areas of knowledge; and there is developed a succeeding generation of teachers to carry the torch forward.[8]

[8] See the excellent article by Buell G. Gallagher, "The Necessity for Federal Aid to Students in Higher Education," *Educational Record*, Vol. 31 (1950) pp. 46–49.

XV.
Extracurricular Activities

CROWDING OUT STUDIES

And yet he semed besier than he was.

CHAUCER, Prologue to *Canterbury Tales*

A TYPICAL American college or university has within it a veritable horde of extracurricular activities. Look at the yearbook published by the students of any institution and you will see how many and how diverse these are. I am not now speaking particularly of the various athletic sports; they are discussed in another chapter. It may be well, however, to enumerate these in passing—football (the varsity, the second team, and the freshman squad), crew, baseball, basketball, track and field sports, tennis, rugby, soccer, swimming, boxing, wrestling, and gymnastics.

Besides athletic sports there are the college daily newspaper, the literary magazine, the annual, the college comic publication, debating (varsity, second team, and freshman), student-body government (including the activities of its officers and its executive, welfare, and special committees), class government (senior, junior, sophomore, freshman), yell leading, athletic managerships, dramatics, scholarship societies (Phi Beta Kappa, Sigma Xi, Tau Beta Pi, and a bevy of imitations in the several schools and colleges), honor societies in each college class (in recognition of work in student activities), chess, singing societies (for men

134

and for women), and the organizations which relate to the work of virtually each of the collegiate departments. Some of these enumerated activities are closely connected with the academic work of the college; they are based on marked success in scholastic activities and are designed to stimulate further discussion of the work in which the student is engaged. In the proper sense of the term these are not extracurricular. Nor should the religious organizations of students be placed in the extracurricular class; for they minister to something which mankind regards as essential and yet in many institutions is not touched by the college itself.

But the great mass of them are properly named as activities outside the curriculum. Unquestionably they have value. In the first place, the student who takes part in them has to work with other students and learn how to get along with them. This is an important lesson to learn for life in human society. He feels, too, a sense of personal responsibility (yes, and of individual importance) which may easily be lacking in classroom work. He has a job to do; others will decide whether it is well or ill done. If it is a debate, not only the judges but the audience will pass judgment. If it is an article in the daily, the editor and, later, all readers will see it and act as critics. What the individual does will attach itself specifically to him and will win far greater attention than a classroom exercise. It calls, too, for individual initiative. All this is certainly not to be censured; indeed, it is beneficial.

However, the various factors that give it value are also bases for its becoming an abuse. Because a larger group will read what a student author has written, and many more will hear the debater than a recitation of his in any classroom, and because the importance of the individual is stressed, he will naturally and inevitably tend to place work on extracurricular activities ahead of his academic work, and attend to his studies in the intervals of time remaining. The very fact that initiative is possible, and that it is prized, will cause the student-body official to spend endless hours in discussion of student-body problems and seek some new and original way to solve some difficulty of long standing. The larger the student body, the more numerous are the problems that arise, and the more time therefore must be given to the discussion and transaction of its business.

Besides, in all these fields the element of competition enters. The president of the junior class, for example, may have his eyes on the student-body presidency. He must therefore make an outstanding success of his present position, or at least must build up publicity for himself. In dramatics there is naturally an eagerness to be advanced from a walking part to a lead, and this means excelling the throng of others who have similar ambitions. Those who start as cub reporters on the daily hope to attain the editorship. Competition exists in each and every one of these fields. What is the inevitable result? One must work harder on his debates, his acting, his reporting, than others do; he must do a better job, and naturally this means spending more and yet more time. It is said of at least one college daily that when promotions on the staff are under consideration careful note is taken of the precise number of hours each competitor has worked. Whether this is literally true is unimportant;

in spirit it is true. The competition is so intense that each who strives spends more and yet more time on his chosen activity.

As a result, not only does actual college work become subordinate, but even in conversation and in thought the extracurricular activity has first place. I can recall an occasion when a student asked the professor in whose class he appeared on a Friday morning to excuse him as unprepared; he explained that he had participated in an interclass debate the night before and could not direct his thoughts to his studies. Imagine what goes on in the mind of an intercollegiate debater on the night of the contest against his college's leading rival. How much time and thought will he be able to give to his work on Milton or on the history of the Middle Ages?

There is in many ways a great similarity between the valid criticism of athletics and the criticism applicable to other extracurricular activities. Of their intrinsic value there is no doubt; but they are overdone, they are carried to extremes, and tend to push out of their proper place the academic pursuits of the college. This overzealousness is intensified by the esteem in which these activities are held, both on the campus and in the outer world. That a young man has been student-body president or editor of the college daily gives him a good deal of publicity while he is in college, and in his home town the local newspaper will dwell upon this important fact repeatedly. If he belongs to a fraternity or club and successfully represents it in any sort of competition, his fame will be heralded not only in the chapter bulletin, but in the national publication of the fraternity as well. Compare all this with what happens to the student elected to Phi Beta Kappa: his name is listed once, and only once, in small type in the college newspaper, and once in the annual. To be sure, he wears the key. But so far as campus fame is concerned, there is no comparison between the shining glory won by a leading actor, politician, or editor, and the infinitesimal flicker of a sparkle on a Phi Bete key.

The difference does not end at that point. When the twain leave college and go into the world, the presidency of a student body is regarded by society as a whole as a far greater recommendation than the symbol of high scholarship. As I have watched college graduates, I have been acutely conscious of the fact that college prominence "pays"; the captain of the varsity track team can usually find a job, and a good one, because his name is well known, quite aside from the fact that his employer may be an athletic "fan." When, therefore, in discussions of the comparative value of such activities, it is pointed out that campus heroes have attained this or that post after graduation, it is interesting to ask oneself whether the campus prominence was not partly or wholly the cause. If scholastic success were to be given the publicity that extracurricular activities now have, one wonders whether the honors graduate might not be chosen, rather than the track captain.

Some years ago, at the University of California, a graduate student in education worked on a very interesting problem.[1] He wanted to find out what type of undergraduate career led to success in later life. He

---

[1] George Lawrence Maxwell, "A Method for Studying the Relation between Types of Undergraduate Collegiate Life and Post Collegiate

chose five classes (1900–1904) which had graduated somewhat more than twenty years earlier, on the theory that by the time of his investigation it should be possible to determine who had made a success. He circularized a number of members of each class, asking each to name those of his classmates who in his judgment had been most successful, and pointing out that the term "success" should be interpreted in the broadest sense. The results of the questionnaires were then tabulated, and those who had been named by more than one person in each class were listed. A study was thereupon made of the college careers of the members of these five groups. Those who combined distinguished scholarship and some student activity led all the others—which is not surprising, since they had demonstrated not only intellectual qualities, but also an ability to work successfully with others and the possession of qualities of leadership. Men of this type have been chosen as the Rhodes Scholars. Yet in connection with the selections for these scholarships it has been pointed out: "In any case, too great participation in extracurricular activities may deprive a gifted man of the opportunity of getting the solid intellectual training upon which leadership in the modern world must inevitably be based."[2] The success attained by former Rhodes Scholars in numerous aspects of American life proves the merit of the criteria employed in the selections.[3]

Performance," unpublished dissertation, 1925. Mr. Maxwell died all too early while serving as Dean of Administration at the University of Denver.

[2] Frank Aydelotte, *The American Rhodes Scholarships* (Princeton University Press, 1946), p. 22.

[3] *Ibid.*, pp. 20–48 and 81–106.

There is one point that it is well to stress. The graduate of 1900 judges these activities on the basis of his experience of fifty years ago. He does not realize how, especially in the large universities, the competition in each activity has increased and the time and energy consumed are vastly greater than in those simple days of the beginning of the century. A student-body presidency today leaves but little time for serious attention to studies; it is a matter for surprise when a student holding this post also attains academic honors.

In short, we concede the value of these various activities but maintain that they are being carried to such extremes that they become obstacles to the educational aims of the college. If it be retorted, "But through his student-body presidency John secured an education far better than any that History or Chemistry or French could have given him," I should reply: "Then why do we have colleges and spend great sums upon them? Why didn't John go to work instead of to college and join the Elks or Rotary or any one of the countless other organizations that American life has created, serving on its various committees and striving to climb up the ladder of its offices? This would have given him experience similar to that which he has had, and he would simultaneously have been earning a living. Nor would he have had to give a thought to college classes." It is hard for an outsider to realize how hectic the life of a "big man" on a college campus is. His days are filled with committees, conferences, presiding at meetings of this, that, and the other, political caucuses, and a round of activities which are so many and so varied that his attendance at classes tends to be just as little as will permit him merely to get by.

140

Extracurricular Activities

There is no doubt of the lure that these activities have. This may not be so important when a young man or woman of mediocre intellect dissipates his energies in debating or journalism or dramatics or even less intellectual activities such as selling copies of the college magazine on the street like a newsboy. The great harm is done when a fine mind is diverted from university pursuits to spend his time in such activities. To be sure, he can, in spite of this, make a passing grade in his studies. This means doing no more than is absolutely necessary to secure "C" grades. For him, studies become an interruption in the really interesting activities of the campus.

May I illustrate by the example of a young man, well known to me, who was editor of the campus daily, a member of the executive committee of the student body and, in general, what is known as a "BM" (Big Man) on the campus? He never was in danger of flunking a course, and without exertion got a passing grade in all of them. But he was equally in no danger of graduating with honors or being elected to Phi Beta Kappa. On the receipt of his bachelor's degree he entered law school; extracurricular activities were automatically and necessarily cast aside. And he graduated from the school as the first man in his class. Is it not pathetic that one destined to become a leader in his profession gained so little from the studies assumed to be foundational to his specialization? He could and would have been an outstanding student in his undergraduate days if he had not spent so much of himself on matters which unquestionably have value but which certainly do not equal the highly important studies which he neglected.

141

The Greeks, as usual, had a phrase for it; it is μηδὲν ἄγαν ("nothing too much"). We have abused these activities as we have abused athletics, and made education but a sort of backwall to the activities of the hero performing under the Klieg lights of college prominence. A halt must be called; the activities must take their proper place and not crowd their way to the fore, displacing academic pursuits.

Our competitive spirit has gone so far that our debating teams must tour the country to meet teams representing colleges large and small, even as in football there is a veritable ladder of contests (within each conference) leading up to the dazzling height of a bowl game. To all this has now become attached the characteristically American practice of holding conventions. There are college journalistic conferences, there are football conventions, there are meetings of student-body officers. And I suspect that college dramatics will follow the same course, as fraternities and sororities have done these many years. One wonders how valuable most of these meetings are.

In extracurricular activities the solution is like that for athletics, a greater number of participants with a lessening of the competitive spirit. More debates, more plays, more persons on committees—but less time to be devoted to them by each participant. This seems to me wise not only for those who are today overdoing these activities, but also for the many who are introverts and need just such participation to round them out. In other words, we should create in extracurricular activities the amateur rather than the professional spirit.

Extracurricular Activities

The administration of the college or university has no right to close its eyes to the existing situation. It should neither permit a boy to be flunked out of college because of excessive participation in these activities, nor, above all, allow a youth of intellectual ability to be diverted from academic pursuits through absorption in these rivals of theirs. The administration has an obligation which it must not shirk. The appointment of a faculty adviser in each field, whose business it should be to prevent both of these catastrophes, would be worth trying. It would not be the advisers' function to act as censors of student activities; they should not forbid a debate on a particular subject, or criticize student editors for a specific article or editorial; but they should make it their primary business to see that these activities do not usurp so much of a student's time as to interfere with the primary purposes of the institution. At the same time, a definite limit should be placed on the number of activities in which a student may take part, the number of offices he may hold. Other methods of meeting the problem will doubtless suggest themselves. At any rate, the college must put an end to the abuse of these activities which undoubtedly exists today.

XVI.

Athletics

IN THE HEADLINES

And all the sport is stale, lad.

KINGSLEY, *The Water-Babies*

THE ASPECT of college life which makes the deepest impression on the public is athletics. Of all its forms, football of course is king, though basketball is now also forging to the front. In some institutions crew is even more highly regarded. Track and field sports command much attention. Next probably comes baseball, followed by tennis. Swimming and boxing are less in the public eye. No one need be told of the way these sports are esteemed. Football draws crowds of 80,000, 100,000, or even more at the games climaxing the season. Betting is rife. On such occasions, and such alone, can great groups of alumni be assembled. As a result, class reunions are most often held on the night before the Big Game.

A winning team is lionized. Service clubs give them dinners, celebrating their achievements, and prizes if they become "champions." But woe betide them if the team has a losing streak. Past victories will be forgotten, and only their failures remembered. The worst fate of all will face the coach. His previous successes, even for a series of years, will not avail him. The alumni wolves will descend upon the athletic board and demand his blood. "The coach must go," will be

144

the cry. Even where a contract with him has still several years to run, and it will cost the college or its student body thousands of dollars to purchase a release, there is no diminution in the demand for his removal.

The boys who play on the teams are confronted by many difficulties. First of all, they are college students, and presumably—though not always—they are seeking an education. They therefore have their classes to attend, their laboratory work to perform, their papers to write, their reading to complete. Football practice, during the season, calls on a boy's time from 3:30 to 6:00 P.M. Then comes the training table, followed by "chalk talks" by the coaches. By the time ten o'clock arrives he is dog-tired, fit only to roll into bed. If to this is added the necessity of earning funds to pay his fees and his board and room and other expenses, it is difficult to see how any save an exceptional individual can bear all these burdens.

The fact is that various underhanded devices are not infrequently employed. An alumnus or a backer of the college (who may never have trodden a college campus save en route to an athletic contest) may lend the student athlete several thousand dollars and "forget" that the "loan" has been made. The college or its student-body officials may find a not too arduous but well-paying job for him. There have frequently been references to such employment as "winding the college clock." President Carter Davidson of Union College declared that money paid to athletes should be for "genuine work—and not farcical clockwinding or turning out the lights." He also stressed that athletes should not secure protection "by taking pseudo-courses in athletic methods in which he is automatically given high grades."[1] George Modlin, President of the University of Richmond, says frankly: "It is impossible for a student to play football, spend sufficient time in study to make satisfactory grades, and at the same time work in a job at normal wages to pay his room and board. There simply is not enough time in a school year to do so, even if a sufficient number of jobs were available."[2] There are undoubtedly some institutions which go further and actually pay their athletes. The football coach at the University of Nevada spoke openly on this matter to the regents of the institution. He said: "Good football players want plenty these days. As an example: I offered a few junior college transfers in California board, room, tuition, books, transportation, and even $50 a month, and I never even heard from them. I offered some other boys scholarships to play football and they told me personally and quite frankly that they could do better elsewhere."[3]

On the academic side, the most athletically-minded colleges permit their athletes to glide through their courses with a minimum of effort. A professor in one college said that it was "as much as his job was worth" to flunk a varsity football player. The president of a university spoke to me in high terms of his gridiron squad, saying however that he had only one criticism to make of them, namely, that they didn't attend classes often!

[1] *San Francisco Chronicle*, December 14, 1949.

[2] *Time*, January 1, 1951, p. 36. Quoted by courtesy of *Time;* copyright Time Inc., 1951.

[3] *San Francisco Chronicle*, February 19, 1950.

Do not think that all this is merely the wail of a pro-fessor in an "ivory tower." Listen to the formal recommendations of the National Association of Collegiate Commissioners, the men in charge of the ten athletic conferences of the universities and colleges of the country. They urged "that the public, alumni and others recognize that the continued existence of college athletics depends upon the maintenance of a sane and sound balance in the life of the student athlete under which he must be a student primarily and an athlete incidentally." Their specific recommendations were:

1) "Definite restrictions upon, or elimination of out of season practice in all sports, particularly spring practice in football and basketball.

2) "Curtailment of sports schedules to a more limited number of games, and to the avoidance of overlapping of seasons in the various major sports.

3) "The preservation of institutional control of athletics free from the interference of outside pressure groups, including those of alumni or other groups."

The Commissioners speak of the "disproportionate pressures which are building up in college athletics generally and on the student athlete in particular." They recommended "that the colleges take steps again to bring athletic activity into proper perspective and balance in relationship with the academic and other phases of college life."[4]

It is significant that sensible sports writers are acutely aware of the evils in intercollegiate sports, primarily football. Thus Will Connolly writes in the *San Francisco Chronicle:* "Unless the faculty steps in

[4] *San Francisco Chronicle,* July 24, 1951.

147

and rescues the lad from the clutches of the coach, he's destined to spend two-thirds of the scholastic year practicing or playing a game." And he says even more directly: "It's about time the sport was restored to the control of classroom profs, as distinguished from coaches. The profs—and prexies particularly—will have a lot to answer for if they don't put a firm foot down."[5]

Assuredly, false standards are created by this glorification of athletics. When a touted high school athlete enters as a freshman, the newspapers make special news of it. All through their lives, star athletes are regarded as "newsworthy"; whatever they do will be published with a recollection that John Doe was the famous halfback of such and such a college from 1912 to 1915. As President-Emeritus Hughes of Iowa State University correctly says, "Success in football, unsupported by high grades, is more likely to lead to success in professional football than to success in law, medicine, or business."[6]

And even the authorities of the college play their part in distorting the place of athletics in the institution. I recall that when a college trackman broke the world's record in the hundred-yard dash, some years ago, newspapers published his picture along with that of the president of the college, and the latter was represented as saying: "X has done more for the college than anyone has ever done." On another occasion the trustees of a college, on recommendation of the president, formally voted congratulations and best

[5] June 4, 1951.
[6] *A Manual for Trustees of Colleges and Universities* (Iowa State College Press, 1945), p. 120.

wishes to their athletes who were about to engage in a national competition; one doubts whether many congratulatory resolutions have been adopted for scholars who have attained high honors or made outstanding discoveries. A college president may omit to attend debates or plays in which his students participate, but think of the furor that would be created if he failed to attend the Big Game.

I do not wish to be misunderstood. I believe that sports are admirable; they build up the body and play a part in developing valuable qualities in human beings. It is their distorted place in college life to which I object. I feel, too, that their influence, not only on the student body as a whole, but on the competitors, is bad. An immature boy of eighteen to twenty-two is made so much of on the campus, so cheered at rallies, so highly regarded by his fellows, and, above all, given such prominence in the press, that he is indeed a rare youth if his head is not turned. I am confident that a varsity hero gets more inches of space in the newspapers while playing on his college team than he will receive all the rest of his life. "Dink" Templeton, journalist and former Stanford track coach, ascribes the lure of professional football to a number of causes, among them being this: "Once you get a taste of those headlines and being a big shot in your own city, it's like a drug you can't give up."⁷ And, of course, if an education is really important, the athlete has failed to obtain what he should get out of college because football practice and "success" have loomed far larger than any academic course. To be sure, some athletes have

⁷ *Fortnight: California's Own Newsmagazine*, Los Angeles, February 27, 1948.

been able to live down their athletic fame and have
made successes as physicians or lawyers or even
scholars. But these are, I believe, the exceptions.
Moreover, it must be remembered that athletic competition has increased manyfold in intensity during
recent decades and what has proved true of those
earlier gladiatorial heroes will, in all probability, not
be as true of the present-day athletes.

The effect on the campus is bad; students feel that
attendance at a football game is imperative, while
musical productions, dramatic performances, and lectures may be sparsely and even discouragingly attended. And unquestionably no other college honors
are as highly regarded as winning the Big W or the
Big S or whatever letter may represent the college
athletically. Besides, these contests lead to an absurd
show of hatred between institutions, with rowdyism
and secret attacks on the other campus, lawn-burning
and paint-splashing and the like, as the inevitable results. At times the student body really runs amok and
burns and destroys.

The general public regards these contests as gala
occasions, comparable to circuses and prize fights; one
can take his wife there, or his best girl, and get a thrill
out of the crowd, the bands, the "Star-Spangled Banner," and the card stunts. And when it is over, they can
crowd the cafés and toast the victors and taunt the
losers.

It means, too, that colleges are judged by the public
according to their athletic successes. Many a college
or university which has the lowest of academic standards looms large in the newspapers through its prowess
with the pigskin and by some strange process of

thought is considered one of the country's outstanding institutions. Very few students have the good luck in the universities publicized for their athletic prowess that Christian Gauss's anonymous student had: "There were three of them [i.e., institutions] that I heard about particularly, Yale and Harvard and Princeton, not because they were the best universities, but because their athletic teams received most space in the sporting columns that came under my eye."[8]

All too often at least one of the contending teams in the various annual bowl games represents a college which would not by any chance be regarded as among the leading forty, fifty, or even one hundred colleges, on the basis of scholastic standards. As a result, probably many a boy, partly lured by the athletic success of the institution, partly deceived by the newspaper publicity into thinking it a really first-rate college, is enticed into entering a college of the third or fourth class. I am particularly sorry when the boy thus beguiled is of intellectual promise. Of course, I readily agree that no institution, however poor, can keep a real student from succeeding in making himself a scholar. But think how much less he gets than he might have gained in a superior college.

And more and more in recent years has the American desire to determine the precise ranking of each team, and the championship of an area, led to interstate and interregional contests and a plethora of bowl games. In tennis, the players must be ranked in order nationally. The sports writers still debate whether Michigan or Notre Dame was the best football team of the year 1948. Who is best? second? third?—these

[8] *Through College on Nothing a Year*, p. 2.

questions come constantly to the fore. Surely all this is more in harmony with gambling instincts than sport for its own sake, for cultivating a good physique, for inculcating true sportsmanship.

What can be done to prevent the octopus from sucking more and more of the life of our colleges and universities? First and foremost, the bowl competitions, which bring together teams from widely sundered parts of the country, have no excuse for existing save the desire to make more and yet more money and the yearning of the public to learn whether team A in one region is better than team B in another. Neither aim is worth consideration.[9] In the second place, there should be far more in the way of intramural sports; these should be given every encouragement as attracting more and more students to physical development. Third, trips for athletic purposes should be steadily reduced. In practically every area there are colleges enough whose teams would give sufficient competition. As matters now stand, after the football season opens on or about September 15, there is a game, and with a tough competitor, every Saturday till the so-called Big Game, at the very end of November. This is too hard a schedule for anyone, certainly for young men whose primary purpose is educational. And if the team has the "good fortune" to play in a bowl game, the season is extended till January 1. This means that

[9] Bowl contests are well discussed by Will Connolly, sports writer in the *San Francisco Chronicle* (September 3, 1951): "There is no denying that the original bowl was a commercial or real estate enterprise, and the multiplicity of latter-day bowls serves the same purpose. . . . A game on January 1—six weeks after well-behaved conferences have closed their books—is a circus stunt and in no way an integral part of football."

there is football competition throughout virtually the entire academic semester.

I know that the spectators have become so absorbed in football throughout a season that they would resent it if some of the closely fought contests with teams that come from a distance of a thousand miles or so were taken from them. They love the stadium in much the way the ancient Romans loved the Coliseum. "To the lions!" may not be on their lips, but "Fight harder!" is the modern equivalent, and shouts of "Kill him!" from the grandstands are by no means unknown. The public would feel deprived of a show, a circus, to which they have looked forward. Then let them go if they will—and in ever larger numbers—to the professional football games. In short, we must make college athletics less of a public spectacle, less of a wandering circus; we must keep it at home in two senses, within the campus itself and within its immediate environs. If this policy of moderation does not succeed or if public pressure is able to break it down, then I should prefer to follow Chancellor Hutchins and give up intercollegiate football altogether. The Massachusetts Institute of Technology has entirely abandoned it. Neither Chicago nor M.I.T. has gone out of business academically. The truth which universities seek to find and teach is not subserved by the shouting mobs in athletic stadiums.

Bad as the effect is on the athletes themselves and on the public attitude toward colleges and universities, doubtless even worse is the effect on the entire student and alumni bodies. The athletic hero is frantically applauded, regarded as far more important than any other student, whether he be a brilliant scholar, a college editor, or even a student-body president. As great athletic contests approach, their probable outcome is the constant subject of student-body discussion on the campus, at every fraternity, sorority, and boardinghouse. College songs fill the campus, the team is constantly cheered and its members are interrogated on a vast number of details of the coming struggle. College courses are disagreeable interruptions in this athletic furor. Homecoming celebrations for alumni are arranged at the time of the Big Game. Classes are unofficially dismissed for this important intellectual activity. And when the day of the great event actually arrives, the atmosphere is electric. The town is crowded early with people of all kinds, including throngs of the fair sex. Streets are packed, rooters' hats are to be seen everywhere, bands add to the din. Hawkers cry programs, flowers with the colors of the opposing colleges, emblems of the rival institutions. Finally, amid tense excitement the fray begins, and all too often the attitude of the crowd takes one back centuries to the ancient gladiatorial conflicts. The loss of a yard causes a moan. When the score is close, booing of opposing players and shouts denouncing the officials are to be heard. The worst in human nature tends to creep out—over what? Whether a pigskin is to cross a certain line or not. Supposedly intelligent men and women lose their dignity and their sanity and act as though the fate of a nation were at stake. I fear that few of them felt as deeply when the fine democracy of Czechoslovakia was crushed beneath the Communist heel.

In short, a totally false point of view exists on our campuses. Intellectual institutions in the eyes of all too many have become schools for training and cheering athletes. Colleges founded by earnest, God-fearing men and women who gave what little they had to bring the light of education to youth, have become something very different, and education has been pushed into a place far inferior to tackling and blocking and punting. The people of our various states furnish money gladly to their universities and colleges, but their aim is to educate and to train, not to have boys and girls put on monkey caps and yell their lungs out because a ball was pushed forward a yard.

What does the athlete gain from his career? How many great athletes have had notable successes in later life? Statistics should be most carefully scrutinized. If a minor athlete subsequently gains a distinguished place in the world, the fact that he was an athlete is heralded far and wide. The real question, however, has to do with the first-string men, those who play day after day and receive columns of publicity. And I am talking of such a game as football, not tennis. Of the latter it can be said that it does not require nearly the time that football does, it does not set the campus, the alumni, or the community in a state of frenzy, and consequently does not produce columns of publicity and streams of pictures.

In all honesty, I do not for a moment imagine that what you have just read will cause radical changes in college athletics. Too much money is involved in them, too many people enjoy the thrills of the games, to permit athletics to sink back into its proper place. But the facts are as I have stated them, and the recent scandals in basketball in which certain players from Long Island University, New York City College, Manhattan

College, and Bradley University were bribed to "throw" games or "fix" the number of points in those in which they participated, cast a veritable blaze of light on the situation in major college sports. No one offers proof that football games have been "fixed," or "thrown," but what reason is there to believe that football players, too, may not have been bribed? Since gambling on basketball games was the soil in which this scandal grew, may not gambling interests, certainly no less active in such sports as football, have succeeded in winning over players in these sports as well, to do their bidding? Listen to what Clarence Price, veteran basketball coach at the University of California, said of "high-pressure proselyting methods used to induce athletes to college: 'Some alumnus goes all out, and pays a lot of dough to a high school kid, and maybe gives him a car—all against the rules—and what can you expect when some shady character approaches him? The basketball player probably feels he's gone that far, he might as well get all he can.' "[10] What is there in this statement which might not be true in other sports as well? Of course, the boys found guilty will be punished; I trust the briber will not escape. But beyond this what steps have the colleges taken to extirpate an evil which is implicit in the present system? It takes courage, a readiness to resist pressure, but the situation which has been revealed should be a sufficient incentive to officials to act. Is the stigma attached to the lives of these college basktball players worth a single basketball game? Better abolish any game, as an intercollegiate sport, when professional gambling attaches to it.

[10] *San Francisco Chronicle*, February 21, 1951.

Long after this chapter was written there arose a veritable tornado of violent criticism of collegiate football as it is played today. There are, for example, the two column editorial in *Life* (Vol. 31, No. 12, p. 38; September 17, 1951), the article in the *Atlantic Monthly* (Vol. 188, No. 4, pp. 27–33; October 1, 1951) by a prominent football player at an important university, revealing the results of the pressure for victory, and the accounts in many newspapers of the scandal at William and Mary College. Even the moving pictures have taken up the theme in "Saturday's Hero."

Especially significant is the report of the faculty of William and Mary College issued in September, 1951, with reference to the athletic situation in that institution:

"Steadily and inevitably, the intercollegiate athletic program has usurped a dominating position in the college. . . . It has become a commercial enterprise demanding winning teams at any cost, even the cost of dishonest academic practice. It has demanded that admission requirements be lowered, and sometimes dispensed with, so that promising athletes can be given the respectability of college enrollment. Limited scholarship funds which should aid young men and women of intellectual promise . . . must go to athletes whose sole recommendation for such aid is their athletic prowess.

"Once on the college rolls, the athletes must somehow be kept there. Their schedules must be arranged without reference to the normal procedure leading to graduation, but rather to enable them to meet the minimum requirements. . . . Courses most vital to the attainment of the educational ideal of the college are avoided in the search for the easy course. . . . There is pressure for special consideration for athletes on the score of heavy athletic duty. The tragic consequence is illustrated by the graduation records of the past nine years; football players as a group have been only a little more than half as successful as the rest of the student body in completing the requirements for the degree. They have been exploited on the gridiron under the pretense of being educated.

"We have seen this athletic program vitiate the most elementary standards of honesty and right conduct . . . ravage the morale of our student body." The faculty confessed "our share of responsibility for having failed hitherto to halt the insidious growth of these evils." But they declared their intention to assume in the future complete control of the entire athletic program, making it "a beneficial but distinctly subordinate activity of the college."

XVII.
Fraternities and Sororities

THEIR GOOD AND THEIR EVIL

A man's a man for a' that.

ROBERT BURNS

FRATERNITIES and sororities exist on most college campuses. They are usually branches of national organizations, though there are also local groups. Members reside in a fraternity or sorority house which is generally filled to overflowing; in that way the house obtains more income for running expenses, and to pay off the inevitable mortgage—for all too often fraternities have built houses more costly than they could afford and as a result are plunged headlong into debt.

In fraternity and sorority life there are undoubted advantages. First of all, the house provides living quarters shared with a presumably agreeable and congenial group. Then, too, the older members are interested in giving the initiates whatever information they consider helpful to one embarking on a college career. Besides, the tie is one that continues after graduation, and the reunions assemble those with whom one has lived in close and friendly association as a student. The alumni, too, include numerous persons with whom contact is pleasant and frequently helpful; the fraternity bond may be a passport to the business or professional world. Life in the fraternity brings the members into close contact with a few of the faculty

159

who are members of the organization. It rubs the rough edges off the boys who have had few advantages and teaches some of the social amenities. Moreover, its expressed ideals are high. These are among the benefits to those who join the organization; they are indisputable.

Each year, the chapter (as the local branch is called) engages in "rushing" likely "material"—inviting recruits to replace members who have graduated or for other reasons have left the college. Most often the chapter seeks freshmen who, of course, will presumably remain four years in college and the fraternity and gradually become leaders.

The processes of "rushing" vary. In some institutions, very wisely no student can be "pledged" to a fraternity or sorority until he has been one full year in college. This gives the student a chance to devote himself to his college work without the distractions of "rushing" or the special tasks that fraternities impose on freshmen. Besides, the new student has a chance to "size up" fraternities in general, and in addition find out the characteristics of the several fraternities, and decide whether he cares to become a member. He can learn which stand scholastically highest, which emphasize athletics or other college activities, what the financial status of the chapter is, what its general tone and what its moral atmosphere are. And the fraternity in its turn will have a far better opportunity to find out what the student under consideration is like and learn his strength and his weakness.

But in other colleges "rushing" takes place in the first few weeks of the academic year. It is a hectic period of crowded engagements for luncheon and dinner, of theater parties, of automobile rides, of excursions to near-by city attractions. Neither candidate nor fraternity is living a normal life; each seeks to put his best foot forward. It is not a good way for a student to be introduced to college life and college studies.

For girls the situation is even worse. Mothers frequently accompany their freshman daughters to the college town and reside with them in a local hotel until the daughters' fates are decided and they go to live in the sorority house—or do not, which is in their eyes a tragedy. Without question, sorority membership—and indeed membership in the "right" sorority—is regarded by the girls as of the utmost importance, and even more by the mothers. There are countless broken hearts when the girl "makes" no sorority, or even when, though successful in "making" some sorority, she fails to "make" the one on which her heart was set. There are gradations in sorority standing.

Selections to sororities are all too often made on the basis of the family's social standing, wealth, or prominence. Of course, the girl's success in student activities in high school and therefore the prospect of similar achievements in college play a part as well. To be sure, a good-looking girl with social graces may well be selected. Scholarship enters into the picture very seldom. Sororities often have teas or receptions to which the mothers of "rushees" are invited, so that the mothers themselves may be scrutinized, and family "background" scanned.

At Stanford University, sororities were regarded as so generally harmful that the trustees, in 1944, voted unanimously that they be discontinued, on the following grounds.

"1. The dual system of responsibility for the housing and social program now in effect is not in the best interests of the women students of Stanford.

"2. This system has caused serious disunity among Stanford women, impairing the University's ability to meet its imperative obligations and responsibilities in respect of women students."[1]

The Board carefully safeguarded "compensation on a fair basis for property rights affected."

Stanford since the time of its foundation had believed it desirable to provide residence halls for women. These halls accommodated some 706 students. Indeed, all women were required to live in them throughout their undergraduate careers unless they became members of a sorority; the sororities had approximately 270 members living in their houses. Accordingly a dual system prevailed at Stanford. Great competition—at times even conflicts—occurred between the two groups. Then too, the evil effect of the rushing season on the girls—not to mention their mothers—was recognized. To put it briefly, the system as it had existed was felt to draw sharp and unnatural barriers between sorority and nonsorority women; unquestionably, unity among the campus women was seriously impaired.

The children of alumni members of fraternities (and sororities too) are in a preferred position; they are known in fraternity language as "legacies." But not infrequently, to the pain of the parents, the son or daughter is rejected. I remember vividly the unhappy experience of a young man, the son of a woman of

---

[1] Annual Report of the President of Stanford University for 1943–44, pp. 15–17.

prominence in the state, who came to the University of California as a freshman and was "rushed" by various fraternities. Not a single one of them offered him a "bid" to join. He ascribed his failure to his lameness, which was conspicuous, and as a result was greatly embittered, and his mother felt equally so. Of course, the lameness may not have been the reason, but the effect on the boy was deep.

Often we do not think of what fraternities and sororities do both to those who are thus "looked over" and discarded and those not even deemed worthy of a cursory glance. Certainly we adults may readily say the whole thing is unimportant and not worth a second thought, but youth is often sensitive and suffers a deep wound when thus "weighed in the balance and found wanting" by the fraternities. Yet years ago President Wheeler made this acute observation: "You can at any time form a better fraternity chapter [from among the nonfraternity men on the campus] than any chapter then in existence." The key to his remark is, of course, the meaning of the word "better."

The final initiation rites are always serious and dignified, but in many fraternities they have been preceded by a so-called "hell week" during which the initiates are subjected to burdensome and disgusting practices; fortunately, the National Interfraternity Conference is making earnest efforts to outlaw it.

When the student is a "pledge," he is driven by fraternity pressure to engage in some student activity. Woe to him if he is interested only in his studies! He must "go out" for yell leader or dramatics or the college paper or, best of all, for some form of athletics. Indeed, the fraternity cherishes on its walls photographs of its members who have gained fame in athletics. At initiation banquets the president of the chapter, in giving a history of its activities during the period just ending, lists the members who have "made the varsity" in football, basketball, and the other most highly regarded sports. Then he will name those who distinguished themselves in minor sports. Next will come the members who have held important offices in the student body or one of the classes. Journalistic honors will next be mentioned. And at the very close, as a sort of afterthought, he will refer to the one member of the chapter who has won the scholastic honors of Phi Beta Kappa, if indeed there was one so selected.

Each house has its own atmosphere. The tendency in fraternities is toward slovenliness and untidiness, characteristic of young men at that age. The conversation does not often deal with serious matters; if it concerns college affairs, it relates to student activities—notably athletics—or possibly a joke from the lecture room. International affairs, critical though they are, do not seem to be of great moment to the fraternity. It is tragic to see a potentially alert mind sunk to this level. It is but fair to say that the National Interfraternity Conference is striving to encourage, in the various chapter houses, discussions of important problems facing the nation.

It is admitted, too, that in general the average of fraternity scholarship is below that of the average of the male student bodies in the various institutions. It was pointed out in November, 1949, at the meeting of the National Interfraternity Conference, that "only 803 out of 2,027 chapters were equal to or above the all-men's average in their respective colleges in the

1947–48 academic year. With 1,224 below that average 'some of the worst' were yet to be heard from."[2] To be sure, it was resolved to encourage good scholarship among the fraternities; we trust it will be more than a mere resolution, as this frank report on the standing of fraternities assuredly is, and should be, most disquieting.

It may be argued, "These are social groups and therefore have the right both to choose such members as they wish and to engage in such discussions as they desire." This I grant; but the college has a responsibility, since these are its students and residence in these organizations is permitted and sanctioned by the college. Where the institution demands that students live in "approved houses," it lists the houses of fraternities and sororities among them. Moreover, these matters of which mention has been made inevitably affect what the student gets out of college.

There is, however, something even more important. I have spoken of some of the affirmative reasons that cause students to be regarded, in fraternity parlance, as "nuggets," that is, for their athletic ability, success in other activities, wealth, social prominence. It is bad enough that college students, presumably in general the pick of their generation, should rate wealth and social standing as of prime importance, that athletic prowess and campus politics should be prized above intellectual power and even character. There tends thus to be developed among fraternity men (and sorority women) a sense of superiority, often a snobbery, that is wholly inconsistent both with a democratic society and with the atmosphere of a true university.

[2] *New York Times*, dispatch from Washington, November 26, 1949.

The implication is: "We are the select ones, the 'upper crust' of the student body." Often in later years the "select" find that they have been outstripped in the race of life by some shabby "barbarian" on whom they looked down during college days.[3]

President Harold Taylor of Sarah Lawrence College attacked the system vigorously on this basis. He said: "The fraternity-sorority values are false, shallow and materialistic. We need a system of residence and community life which retains the attractions of the fraternity house without the snobbery upon which the fraternity house rests. This we can have, if we want it, and if university authorities take the lead in providing it."[4]

There is yet another aspect of these organizations which is most dangerous. They not only choose recruits for unworthy reasons, but they exclude from consideration (at times by provisions in their constitutions) large groups of their fellow students. There is prejudice against Catholics in some of them. Assuredly, though Jews are at times chosen, their religion is a serious handicap. Of course, when a single chapter considers a Negro it causes nation-wide attention. I have been informed that once in a great while a Chinese or a Chinese-American has been selected, but I have not been at any fraternity house where this was done. Likewise, Japanese and Japanese-Americans are automatically excluded. Indeed, it is very seldom that any foreigner (save a Canadian) is invited to join; this bars all students from any other country in the Amer-

---

[3] For an indictment of the fraternity system see *Collier's*, January 8, 1949, pp. 9 and 65, and January 15, 1949, pp. 34–35.

[4] *New York Times*, December 4, 1949.

icas, all from Europe, Asia, and Africa. Some fraternities, to be sure, are participating in the program of international exchange by furnishing hospitality, in the form of board and room, to foreign students. This is good as far as it goes, but aside from the fact that by no means all fraternities and sororities take part in the plan, it is to be noted that these foreigners are but guests, not members. In short, our "best young men and women," so called, hear addresses and read articles emphasizing human brotherhood and decrying prejudice—and yet they make the barriers an intrinsic part of their college lives.

Think what it would mean in international relations if some Latin-American, or Oriental, or European, later destined to become an important figure in the life of his nation, had been made to feel fully a part of a fraternal group and had cemented a friendship with an American who in like manner subsequently attained a post of national importance in our land! Think what it would mean if they could deal with each other on terms of intimacy! On the other hand, how Hitlerian an attitude is created in these young people when they automatically bar from all consideration those of foreign birth, of certain faiths, and of other colors. Fraternities and sororities are thereby forces opposing democratic ideals and indeed the very precepts on which Christianity rests. They plant and water the seeds of intolerance.

Inevitably, this undemocratic atmosphere in which they have lived throughout their four college years cannot help exerting a powerful influence on them when they leave college. It is not too much to believe that the prejudices which lead the most prominent social clubs to erect bars against Negroes, Orientals, and Jews are in considerable part the outcome of what these men (yes, and women) learned to accept as proper and desirable in their college days. The extreme in this respect is reached when some University Clubs, made up entirely of college and university graduates, put up the barriers. The purpose of these clubs is presumably to band together the intellectually elite (but God forbid that their skins should be black or their creed that in which Jesus was born). And they are potent influences in a community. The friendships made within them play a part in countless activities in which the citizenry participates. They form a second wall backing up the fraternity wall, to shut out "inferiors." One is cynically amused when he notes now and then that men and women, members of these "exclusive" clubs, are at the same time active in Brotherhood movements. Their hearts beat with fraternal affection at meetings of Brotherhood organizations, and then without compunction they mount the steps of their brownstone clubs from which many of the brothers with whom they have just met would be excluded. I don't think much of an emotion which expresses itself merely in a speech or a resolution but is content to sleep when a really important action might be taken. And so I dare to say that fraternities and sororities not only have false standards, but are breeding places of undemocratic ideals, and that they exert no inconsiderable influence in nourishing intolerance in social clubs when their members leave college.

There are, to be sure, Jewish fraternities and sororities, and Negro fraternities and sororities. One can, of course, well understand how groups excluded from the "regular" fraternities would resort to organizations of their own. But is it not a fact that these fraternities of minority groups serve only to buttress the wall of separation between themselves and the rest of the student body? Is not there a bit of the self-imposed ghetto about them? In any event, they do not solve the fundamental problem, but rather intensify it. They rest on the assumption that the "regular" fraternities naturally draw racial and religious lines.

No one says that the social clubs (as well as the fraternities and sororities) should not choose their members on a basis of quality in the individual. But Roland Hayes or Marian Anderson would honor any society by being members of it; so too would Louis Brandeis or Benjamin Cardozo. Rigid exclusion of any group (whether written in the rules of the organization or operating as a matter of agreed practice) makes words about democracy on the lips of its members mere dust and ashes. The inculcation of such an attitude in college students in institutions supported by the people of the state who are themselves of all colors, ancestries, and creeds, or in those endowed by generous benefactors, at times members of these very excluded groups, and indirectly, too, supported in many ways by the people as a whole, is a blot upon our educational system and an indictment of our colleges.

There are, to be sure, rays of light amid this blackness of intolerance. At the Massachusetts Institute of Technology the chapter of the national chemistry fraternity, Alpha Chi Sigma, preferred to surrender its charter because a bylaw limited membership to non-

Semitic members of the Caucasian race. At Amherst the chapter of the Phi Kappa Psi fraternity in November, 1948, by unanimous vote, pledged a popular Negro student and announced its intention to initiate him. Although there is no clause in the fraternity's constitution barring Negroes from membership, its national executive committee voted the suspension of the chapter. President Cole of Amherst gave hearty approval to the action of the local group and expressed great pride in it. Still more important is the fact that the trustees of the college definitely announced that after February 1, 1951, they would not permit upon the campus any fraternity with a national constitution that set social or religious barriers against the admission of members. The Amherst group, in spite of the action of the national executive committee, initiated the Negro and made of itself a local organization.[5]

Recently, two similar incidents have been reported: a chapter of a fraternity, and of a sorority, sought each to admit a non-Caucasian student, but met the opposition of the national organization. One was at Bowdoin College, where the chapter withdrew from the national fraternity rather than abandon its purpose to admit a Negro student. The other was at Idaho State College, where a girl described merely as Hawaiian was pledged by a sorority; the national officials reportedly sought to bar her, despite the fact that when national fraternities and sororities were chartered at the college it was with the definite stipulation that there be no restriction with respect to race.

[5] See Alfred S. Romer, "The Color Line in Fraternities," *Atlantic Monthly*, June, 1949, pp. 27–31, for an account of the entire affair.

In November, 1949, a most important step was taken by the National Interfraternity Conference in recommending the elimination of restrictive membership provisions by its member organizations. In so doing, it reversed a previous stand to the effect that the controversial issue was "not proper" for its consideration. The recommendatory resolution adopted by the Conference is as follows:

Resolved, That it is the sense of this conference that:

1) It recognizes that many member fraternities have had and now have restrictive provisions.

2) It recognizes that the question is of concern to many interested parties.

3) It calls these facts to the attention of all member fraternities, appreciating that membership is an individual fraternity responsibility.

4) It recommends that member fraternities that do have selective membership provisions consider this question in the light of prevailing conditions and take such steps as they may elect to eliminate such selectivity provisions.

It is perfectly obvious that the question now rests on the action of the national bodies of the fifty-eight fraternities forming the membership of the Conference, and then—even more—on whether this will merely mean a change in the constitutions of the organizations or will actually be translated into the election of persons from groups hitherto barred.

However, the action taken by the Conference means a degree of progress, and for even this much we should be grateful. It is at least a first step and was adopted by a vote of 36 to 3 fraternities, 19 abstaining. This sentiment, representing what is clearly the view of the majority of the fraternities, should begin to crack the shell of discrimination.

Far better, however, than any "fraternity row" is a dormitory system whereby all students live together and associate with one another and intolerance does not intrude. If all students cannot be housed in dormitories, at least let all freshmen be required to live in them, so that they may have at any rate that much of a taste of democratic living. Fraternities do have certain advantages; in the respect here discussed, however, their influence is not only detrimental to those who are members, but to the college itself and ultimately to society as a whole.

To be sure, there have arisen such organizations as Beta Sigma Tau, which at the time of this writing had thirteen chapters; it definitely announces that it is hostile to any form of discrimination, and lives up to its statement. Here and there throughout the country other fraternities opposed to segregation have arisen. This is good and highly to be praised; but I fear that it will by no means solve the problem. The old-established fraternities will look down on these newcomers, and, I think, even make their policy of nondiscrimination a ground for treating them with contempt and an argument against joining them.

The old-line fraternities and sororities must learn democracy both in admission and in spirit; they must cease to think themselves superior, or else American colleges must question their right to exist in an academic community in a free society. Among them there have been so many members of whom I have been fond and whom I have esteemed that I trust they themselves will see the evil in their discriminatory practices and set standards which will be more fitting in an American college.

172

XVIII.
The Large University versus the Small College

MUCH MAY BE SAID ON BOTH SIDES

To compare great things with small.

MILTON, *Paradise Lost*

THE PROPONENTS of the large university and those of the small college are both so ardent in advocacy of the one and the other type of institution that each side often sees no merit—or at least very little merit—in their opponents' choice. I am of course referring to undergraduate instruction, for even in large universities seminars are usually small and, for graduate work, faculty and facilities are available which the small college does not have. Indeed, in the main, the college tries to be just that—an undergraduate institution—and does not seek to rival the university in the graduate field with its multitude of departments, large library, and laboratories. So the question is really, "Which is better for an undergraduate, the small college or the large university?" The truth is that each has advantages which the other lacks.

In the first place, the large university offers instruction in a host of fields which the small college does not pretend to teach. How many colleges give instruction in anthropology or astronomy, bacteriology or biochemistry, Hebrew or Sanskrit, Portuguese or Polish,

173

forestry or architecture? But even in the departments taught, the offerings in the way of courses are meager as compared with those in the universities. If one examines, for example, the list of courses in history or economics in a large university and compares them with those in a small college, the contrast will be glaring. In other words, the special interests of students are far better met in the large institution.[1]

In the second place, the university's faculty will contain some of the most eminent scholars in the nation, and the opportunity of studying under great authorities in the field of one's choice is one of the important advantages offered by the best of the large institutions. Were one to ask where the fifty most distinguished physicists or historians are teaching, it will be found that all of them, or almost all, are members of the faculties of the large institutions. If an examination is made of the list of members of the National Academy of Sciences, it is astonishing how they cluster in the large universities,[2] while the small colleges are but slightly represented. A striking exception is the California Institute of Technology, which stands among the foremost in number of members; it is, of course, far from being a typical small college.[3]

---

[1] It must be admitted that in the main the opportunity of making a choice among the multitude of courses is not utilized by as many students as should do so. They select courses all too often because friends are taking them, or because the hour is a convenient one, or the subject is a popular one, or the instructor is a "good," at least an "interesting," lecturer. But the opportunity to choose in the many fields is available, and the best students take advantage of it.

[2] Harvard, California, and Chicago are notable examples.

[3] The converse, however, is by no means true. There are numerous large institutions which include among their faculty absolutely no members of the National Academy.

Large University vs. Small College

In the third place, the large state universities have a student body representing a cross section of the people of the state. You will find sons of rich parents, and of parents with limited means. The state university student is living with the kind of people who typically make up our society, and not with a selected group. In the colleges, the basis of selection (save for a limited number of scholarship holders) is not merely ability to meet the academic admission standards, but the means to pay the tuition fees (often high, $600 per annum or more) plus the cost of room and board; hence the college is certain to be more expensive than the state university.

In the fourth place, the large institutions attract a very considerable number of students from all parts of the globe. Contact with the foreigner is itself a valuable educational experience.

In the fifth place, the very fact that the institution is large, and that consequently the responsibility for taking action of all kinds rests primarily on the student himself, encourages self-reliance, individual choice, and personal initiative. The student chooses his segment of the institution, be it college, division, or school; he chooses among the courses permissible in his curriculum; he finds (or seeks to find) his own dwelling place; when he is in academic difficulty, he goes in person to his dean for advice; if he is in a bit of a hole financially, he approaches the official in charge of loans and consults him; he realizes that as a result of illness he must reduce his program of courses, and goes to his dean to discuss the matter with him. In a hundred details he is the master of his own fate. I admit that this resembles throwing boys and girls into the water to teach them to swim. Some may not be able to profit by the Spartan treatment. But those who can, have learned one of life's most important lessons, namely, that of self-responsibility.

Now, what has the small college to offer?

In the first place, the student gets to know, in time, a very large proportion of the student body. He does not feel as though he were walking the streets of a strange city, never expecting to see a familiar face. He feels at home among the many students who are his friends or at least his acquaintances.

In the second place, the courses offered are likely to be fundamental ones in each field, and he is not tempted to wander off into insignificant bypaths. He should, therefore, get a better education than many get in the large institutions through embarking on too many and too highly specialized courses.

In the third place, while it is true that almost all the great scholars ultimately teach in large universities, in the course of their careers they often teach in small colleges; the latter then get the benefit, not only of their scholarly attainments, but also of their enthusiasm in the earlier years of their teaching experience. Thus Bryn Mawr College had on its faculty at one and the same time Woodrow Wilson, Paul Shorey the classical scholar (later at the University of Chicago), Edmund B. Wilson the biologist (later of Columbia University), Edward Washburn Hopkins the philologist (later of Yale University), Edward Keiser the chemist, and Charlotte A. Scott the mathematician.[4]

But, aside from this, it is possible to find in most

[4] Ray Stannard Baker, *Woodrow Wilson: Life and Letters* (New York: Doubleday, Page & Co., 1927–1939), Vol. 1, p. 253.

small colleges scholars of ability, and the students come much closer to them than to the eminent men in the large institutions.

In the fourth place, the emphasis in the small college is overwhelmingly on the undergraduate program, and not, as at some of the large universities, on the graduate program. This is certainly to the advantage of the undergraduates.

In the fifth place, good teaching is emphasized more fully as a primary aim of the instructors than it is in the university, where, while good teaching is desired, promotion rests mainly on research and publication.

In the sixth place, in the small college the student can expect more guidance both academically and personally, and gets it. He is not cast adrift to shift for himself, but when he gets into difficulty of one kind or another the college authorities know it and call him to their offices in an endeavor to assist him.

It is clear that each type of institution has its advantages and the drawbacks that accompany those advantages. The quiet elms of a small college with its careful guidance of students are faced by the bronze gates of a large university, from which pour streaming tides of students, filled with life and vitality, but each responsible for his own fate.

Both institutions are valuable elements in our higher educational system; both have significant contributions to make. They are not rivals or enemies, but supplement each other. And the choice between them made by a student and his parents should be made on the basis of individual needs and individual qualities. And, ultimately, we should say with the Romans: "De gustibus non disputandum."

Not infrequently a student combines the two experiences by taking his undergraduate work in one of the excellent small colleges and then going, for graduate or professional study, to a university of distinguished reputation. Often this practice works extremely well, since the student secures the advantages of both types of institution. However, at times the contact with a great scholar in a university, while one is an undergraduate, serves to act as the spark kindling the student's enthusiasm for a particular field. On the other hand, the faculty of the small college may give him greater guidance. The really important thing is that he go to a first-rate institution, be it small or large.

XIX.
Education and Training

Things are in the saddle and ride mankind.

EMERSON

I T WILL BE agreed that it is difficult to hit a bull's-
eye when the marksman shoots at several targets
at once. Many of our universities and colleges have
no clear conception of their targets, or rather, they
have several conceptions and blaze away in all direc-
tions at once. I shall omit mention of numerous announced objectives and confine myself to the two that
are most prominent, education and training. Education is not designed to fit a person to enter upon this
or that profession; it exists for the purpose of broaden-
ing the student's intellectual interests, for giving him
a notion of the important fields of human knowledge,
for teaching him how to reason, how to make wise
judgments. What it does is done for the sake of the
man. Training is preparation directed to a particular
end; it supplies the physician, the lawyer, the archi-
tect, with the tools of their professions.

Education and training are separate and distinct
aims. However, not only is there general confusion in
what is thought and said about them, but college curricula scramble them together. Indeed, I fear that most
people, including students, while talking bravely of
education, really esteem training more highly. "What

179

are you studying for?" is the question that adults commonly ask of college students, from freshmen to seniors. And of course they mean, "What profession or occupation are you being trained for?" I do not wish to imply that law school courses are not helpful to the forming of wise judgments; that would be absurd. But I do say that their primary purpose is to turn out good lawyers, not educated men and women.

The confusion is most obvious in the premedical curriculum, the largest part of which is made up of courses that are prerequisites to the program of the medical school itself; no more than a smattering of other courses is offered. Medical students today are not really being educated; they have no opportunity to broaden their program or to exercise that freedom of choice which is regarded as appropriate in a liberal arts program. To be sure, one understands that long years of preparation are required of a physician, and that the many specializations in medicine are always making further demands on the medical student's time. How to meet this situation, how to save him from too narrow a program, it is not easy to suggest. One would like to see the bachelor's degree—the usual award at completion of an undergraduate program of real education—made the prerequisite for admission to medical schools, and then to require in the programs of the medical schools themselves whatever work in biology, chemistry, and physics is really needed for the medical program but has not been included in the undergraduate curriculum. But that, I fear, would add still more time to the training of the physician, add to the cost of that training, and increase the age at which he can finally begin his practice. A wholly different solution would be to require two years of strictly premedical work for admission to the medical school, with no pretense of educating the students: no degree would be given until they should have earned their M.D. Yet another, and I think better, solution will be proposed later.

In general, I feel that ideally the undergraduate program should provide education, and that training for the professions, including teaching, should be reserved for the graduate schools. Today we are turning out professional men and women who are not truly educated, but who have devoted themselves primarily to acquiring the training that is necessary for their professions.

However, the line between education and training has been broken down not by certain professional schools and colleges alone; in departments which in themselves stress education you will again and again find courses which are not educational in essence, but technical. This is because the members of the departments themselves fail to see the distinction between the two, or rather consider that the "curse" of technical training does not cling to any work they offer. Moreover, it is not always evident that professors think of education as differentiated from training in their fields. The department of English, for example, is quite willing to create and conduct courses for teacher-training, courses in techniques; and, in general, prospective teachers are driven to take courses in methods of teaching this and that subject. In other words, it is not so much additional knowledge in the subjects to be taught that is stressed, but how material suited to high school students shall be presented. This is not essentially different from telling law students how to prepare briefs.

One thing is clear, and that is that we should differentiate sharply between education and training. Certainly, the freshman and sophomore years should in any event be given over wholly to education; this is little enough time for the purpose. Personally, I wish the whole undergraduate period could be set aside for education, and all professional training be kept for graduate study. I realize, of course, that this would lengthen the time of preparation for the professions. If, however, the undergraduate programs were to be educationally sound and broad in the fields of study included, those who succeed in them should, as a result, be a selected group and intellectually more able to complete a solid professional program in a briefer period. But since my suggestion is, I realize, Utopian, let us at least keep the first two years wholly for a real educational program and resolutely exclude from it courses primarily introduced as prerequisite to the major in this or that department. These prerequisites have not only crept under the tent; too often they are making it uncomfortable for the dwellers there. To speak more directly, the prerequisites take up so much of the student's time in the first two years that when they are added to a very small number of basic requirements the student's program is too tightly packed.

A field like engineering would complain loudly at insistence that the first two collegiate years should be given to subjects such as English, history, economics, the basic sciences, and the like; but its own graduates constantly bemoan the absence of opportunities to learn something of these other fields. And if a lawyer must spend seven years in preparation, and a physician eight or more, and a librarian or social service worker five or six, and a high school teacher (in some states) five, it seems absurd that engineering should seek to compress its training into four years; it certainly deserves six years for the kind of engineers the colleges should turn out.

President Wheeler, of the University of California, once said, "It is the mixing of things which is the great evil." This does not mean that training is not both essential and worthy of all respect, but merely that it has a professional or, if you will, vocational goal. I plead then for a Lower Division completely separated from the Upper Division and devoted wholly to education (general education, if you will). Professional work would begin in the Upper Division, or, where possible, only after the bachelor's degree had been earned.

At once I can hear the outcries of my friends in professional fields: "But history is for the future teacher of history just as vocational; so is Latin for the future teacher, or chemistry." This is true, but these subjects have the good fortune of providing education for all, and are not merely a route to a moneymaking occupation for a few. To be sure, a course in modern history is important to the prospective teacher; this does not in the slightest degree detract from its value to all university students, who should know something about it as a background for their lives as citizens in a country which has abandoned the conception of isolationism. That is the kind of distinction I should make. On the other hand, a course in Latin grammar or in historical bibliography is, I should agree, thoroughly vocational, even though a nonprofessional student may profit from it as a nonprofessional student may from a course in criminology.

As matters now stand, there may be technical or vocational courses in any department; so too, in almost any department there may be educational courses. Not only is this true, but the manner in which the course is taught may transform it from one group to the other. Assuredly, however, the more numerous the courses that are created in any department, the more highly specialized they tend to become, the greater the inevitable tendency toward the technical. Far better is it to limit courses to the fundamental and not make students think that, because unit credits are alike, two courses necessarily have equal value educationally. Two kinds of food may cost the same amount, but their effect on the human body will be very different.

Although in this chapter I am dealing exclusively with the colleges, may I take up for a moment the programs of our high schools? Here, too, we find that various aims are mixed: we have the students who are preparing to go to college or university, those who are seeking to acquire a particular skill fitting them to get jobs when they leave high school, those who are just "going to high school" and taking whatever courses are required there, supplemented by courses chosen because they are easy or seem practical or are popular. My interest at the moment is in the college preparatory group, and I feel strongly that our high schools could do more for them than we often see done. The curricula of these students should be pretty definitely prescribed, taking into account, of course, the kind of college the student plans to enter. And the program should be made up of "solids." A "solid" program, with a requirement of high standards of accomplishment, would do much to bridge the gap between high school and college and might well make it possible for college graduation to take place a year or two earlier than at present.

I fully realize the problems that are created by compulsory education laws which virtually make high school attendance mandatory, and which unquestionably dilute the intellectual average in a class. To be sure, we wish to do all we can for those who are not really college timber, but we should not subordinate the interests of the able students to the pace of the academic snails. Surely, in large high schools, college preparatory students can and should be segregated and given a rigorous training. A program of that sort should be made available to all who are intellectually equipped for it. Often, a promising student who had not thought that college was possible for him may be thus discerned and encouraged and helped on to college or university.

XX.
Courses Appropriate and Inappropriate

DISCRIMINATION IS IMPERATIVE

Easy is the descent ...

VIRGIL

IT IS NOT easy to draw the line between courses that are appropriate to a college or university and those that are not appropriate. When the barriers, however, are once broken down, a precedent is established which leads to further and yet further extensions. Should a college or university teach the business (or is it a profession?) of the mortician? Most would, I think, say "No" and argue that instruction of that kind should be given in an institution for the particular purpose. What about the teaching of the beautician's craft? The answer should undoubtedly be the same. It is not the business of a true university to teach these things, not because they are inferior, but because the instruction is merely the teaching of techniques, and it is not the function of the college to teach techniques.

A college is not a trade school; it should not teach how to milk a cow or how to use a typewriter. This does not mean that courses in agriculture or business are inappropriate; but they should be thoroughly scientific courses which teach the principles involved in the various branches of agriculture or business. In these the student does not merely use his hands; he is led to draw judgments on the basis of observations. Likewise in matters pertaining to business. A study of economic theory is appropriate, indeed essential, in a university; so also do the principles of international trade belong in the curriculum.

I do not wish to be misunderstood. There are fields which are perfectly worthy to be taught, and yet not in a true college. A business school (or college, as it prefers to be called) properly gives instruction in bookkeeping, typewriting, shorthand, business forms, the use of business machines, and the like. So, too, does an agricultural school give practical training in subjects of immediate utility to the farmer. The care of cattle, hoeing and planting, rotation of crops—these have their place there, but (note this) they are taught as things to be learned, as things accepted by workers in the field, not as matters the scientific basis of which should be studied and determined.[1]

Perhaps one way to answer the question in the large is to ask oneself whether the field to be taught is a profession. If it is not, then the presumption is that it should be taught in a trade school, not in a college or university. Is hotel management a profession? I sincerely doubt it, and do not for a moment believe that the subject is appropriately included in a university

---

[1] It is easier to draw broad distinctions of this kind than to arrive at a decision concerning particular courses. In what I say here it is not meant or implied that colleges, and especially universities, should not give professional training, but that training of that kind should be given in the spirit of the university, not of the trade school. The medical student, for example, should be taught the technique of dissection as a real part of his scientific training.

curriculum. And even in thoroughly academic departments it is so easy for improper courses to insinuate themselves. A course that is strictly informational is, to say the least, of questionable merit. Courses that are limited to telling students merely what tools to use (whether books or instruments) are not desirable for undergraduates.

However, what I have said is not meant to defend the ancient *status quo* and oppose the introduction of new departments or new courses. The mind of the faculty should be thoroughly open on this point, and it should be remembered that once upon a time the only respectable subjects were Greek, Latin, philosophy, and mathematics. The natural sciences, the modern languages (including English!), the social sciences, the various professional fields (save theology)—not one of these was admissible to the college curriculum. Changes have indeed occurred; progress been made; but, on the other hand, this does not mean that every novelty deserves a place in a college. The subject must not be merely an implement; it must not be something that demands of a student no intellectual effort beyond exercise of his memory, or of a certain knack with tools or equipment. And the established departments should constantly scrutinize their own offerings to see that they do not fall into the same error.

The people as a whole often do not understand this, and certainly special interests will press for courses and curricula in their field. They want trained personnel, and in their trade conventions they stress that their activities are as professional as medicine or law. They want the training given, given preferably in a relatively short time and crowned with a degree. Advertising consultants and realtors, hotel owners and police officials—all alike put on the pressure. And they want the student to learn the mechanics of the craft so that he can enter it fully equipped at the very moment of his graduation. It is infinitely better to give the student a broad education and a trained mind which, after a certain preliminary adjustment, can make its way in a great variety of fields. A law student does not need to be told in law school how to file a legal document; this is something he can learn readily enough. He should concentrate on the fundamentals of jurisprudence. Indeed, a really well-trained student in any worthwhile subject has a background that will permit him, without too much difficulty, to gain a footing in many kinds of work.

Colleges, however, yield all too readily to demands for curricula which are wholly vocational (not professional), because the special interests behind them are vociferous and pushing. Well, the barber performs useful services, but surely training for his work does not belong in a college or university. The pressure to establish new curricula in vocational fields springs in part from the desire of the proponents of these special curricula to crown graduation from them with a college degree. It is the degree that is important; this reveals the esteem in which the public holds them. It sometimes seems as if the public thought more highly of them than the colleges themselves do. The very regard in which degrees are held should lead college faculties to scrutinize with care the manner in which they are granted. Let us not still further devaluate our academic currency.

Indeed, the weakness of many institutions of higher learning is that they multiply courses and at times boast of the number they offer. They fail to see that by so doing they encourage students to take comparatively unimportant courses and thereby crowd out those that are fundamental. It is the quality of the work that counts, not the infinitesimally minute segments of the subject which may be taught in courses. Sometimes it is the fault of an instructor who has written his doctoral dissertation on a minor author or a fragment of history or who has made it the basis of his private research and is eager to give a course on his specialty. But always it must be remembered that courses are given for the benefit of students and that none should be offered that will lead a student to substitute the unimportant for the significant.

In a college in which, in his last two years, a student must complete a major in one of the established departments, the faculty should ask itself, "What ought a student to have studied if he is to be graduated as a major student in this field?" Should a major student in history go forth with but little work in the fields of European history and American history? Indeed, in them there is so much that is really essential that it is hard to get it all into the cup. That being so, the less important (say the history of Mexico) should be rigorously excluded. This does not mean that such courses should not be available, especially for graduate students. But at the same time it must be remembered that intelligent, well-trained students should be able to read the various works on the subject as well, perhaps, as the professor; in short, not everything need be taught in courses.

Courses Appropriate and Inappropriate

To put it a bit differently, the introduction of each new course should be carefully scanned, but with an open mind. It must always be remembered that, if taught, it will inevitably and necessarily replace in the program of many students courses already taught. If it is as valuable and important as they, it should by all means be added. But let the college be sure before it acts. And let it keep resolutely in mind the distinction between a true college course and a trade school course.

XXI.
Education by Degrees

Do not squander time, for that is the stuff life is made of.

FRANKLIN

FAR BE IT from me to say that there should be shorter periods of study for this or that profession. The increasing knowledge in each field makes greater demands on the student preparing for it. On the other hand, as an educated man, irrespective of his particular profession, he should have knowledge and training in many areas of study. He should not go forth merely with his mind stuffed with the technical material of his own field. Inded, he will be the less successful in that field if that is all he knows.

And yet there is another factor that should be considered. All too often, fields of study seek eagerly for the respectability and the equality implied in a degree. It is not so much that the student needs the additional years of study, but that the technical college, as well as the student, yearns for the distinction of a degree. Often this is disguised by the argument that in this field as well a broad educational foundation is desirable; however, when the curriculum is finally enlarged from two to four years, it will usually be found that the additional years have been assigned mainly to subjects leading to the professional courses, at least offered as doing so.

192

May I illustrate the manner in which such extensions may occur? Within various departments of the university there is a group of courses in a field regarded as a subdivision thereof. For example, in English there may be found a few courses in journalism. Gradually this number is increased, and Journalism is separated from English to become a separate department. Then in a short time a whole curriculum is set up containing courses in journalism and other courses as well which have more or less relation to journalism. Next, this is made into a College of Journalism, headed by a professor bearing the additional title of dean; as a college it is granted authority to confer degrees. So the student who has or thinks he has an interest in journalism is encouraged and advised, from the moment he enters the institution, to enroll in the College of Journalism, and his program is in general determined on the basis of preparation for a journalistic life. And if he is really anxious to become a journalist, he is assured that he must secure the degree which will inform the world that he has successfully pursued the full program in the College of Journalism.

It must be considered, too, that a young man or woman thoroughly qualified for the occupation in which training is being given may well find it impossible to pass in college courses such as economics and chemistry, and as a result will be prevented from performing the function in life for which he is really well fitted. Thus in the field of nursing a stiff required preliminary course in college chemistry may prove the hurdle which brings down the candidate and keeps the doors of admission to the profession closed to her.

And yet she may have all the qualities that make a good nurse. Her exclusion may act as a great blow to her ambitions and deny her the opportunity to do the work for which she is best qualified. And thus society loses a potentially valuable servant in a profession of high importance to it.

And, as I have said, I fear it is not so much the desire to give these students a broad general education that prompts the extension of the curriculum, as eagerness to be empowered to grant a degree and to secure equality with other fields of study. All too often a department or college (especially one more or less a newcomer to the academic world) seeks to secure the respect of older departments by demanding, for admission to its senior and junior work, courses that have the reputation of being "tough," even though not really needed for the work in the department.

To be sure, society itself makes much of degrees, and their possession is used as a basis for admission to a large number of fields of work. Do you want to become an officer in the Army? You'd better have a college degree. And this placing of degrees on a pedestal is one of the factors that fill our colleges and universities.

Better far, if degrees are so important, to give them at the end of shorter periods, thereby satisfying the students' desire for the degree and the insistence of the faculty of the particular professional school on equality of status, while at the same time saving the students' precious years. If one does not wish the ordinary degrees to be debased, as it were, human ingenuity should be able to devise others which sound as impressive and justify a gown and a hood.

Education by Degrees

It may be felt that these statements are out of harmony with those I have expressed which favor at least two years of education, preferably four, before entry into professional training. The distinction lies in both the comparative need of basic preparation for the work of the professional school and the time appropriate for preliminary schooling in view of the nature of the profession or vocation. Certainly, two years of general education prior to professional training are always desirable, but certain fields do not appear to require a total of four years training as much as others do. If a student can afford the time and expense involved, by all means let him pursue the longer course; but if this is made an absolute requirement, it may keep out of the field many students who are well adapted to it, and deprive society of services which they are thoroughly competent to render.

The desire to "raise standards" advanced by those who seek to lengthen a curriculum is certainly one with which I am in great sympathy, but this does not always require the addition of a year or two to the period of preparation for a particular field. Standards may be raised through securing better teachers and improving the quality of the work. Let the students work harder instead of working more years.

XXII.
Discussion on the Campus

HOW FREE SHALL IT BE?

Men are never so likely to settle a question rightly as when they discuss it freely.

MACAULAY

IF YOU READ college newspapers, you will find repeated (one might almost say *ad nauseam*) demands that students be permitted to discuss this or that subject on the campus and, above all, to invite speakers whose views represent wide divergences of opinion.

As for discussions by student groups themselves, I feel they should be granted the utmost freedom to deal with any subject whatsoever, under the following conditions: (*a*) that both sides should, of course, be adequately presented; and (*b*) that a due regard should be had for the feelings of this or that other group of students. By the latter statement I do not mean that truth should be distorted or suppressed, but merely that the presentation be such as befits gentlemen and scholars. I see no reason for preventing discussion; indeed, its encouragement is the breath of life of a scholarly institution.

I go further, and say that I see no reason why student groups (groups of and for students exclusively) should not be organized for political purposes. After all, they are going to be American citizens and voters (many of them are already of voting age) and should be encouraged to give thought to the problems of our nation; we want to provide them the opportunity of finding out what they think about these problems in their collegiate days, for thus they will become better citizens, more ready to take an active part in public life. There may well be a Republican Club or a Democratic Club holding its meeting in a campus building. Then it may be asked, "What of a Socialist Club, or a Communist Club?" To the former I would have no objection. As for the latter, I would frankly forbid it to meet on the campus; it is evident that the Communists' first loyalty is to the U.S.S.R., not the U.S.A., and that to judge from what has happened in Czechoslovakia and elsewhere they would overthrow our form of government by any means available.

The action of the trustees of the University of New Hampshire in permitting the full use of campus facilities for political meetings and discussions is, I am convinced, highly to be commended. The statement of policy says: "The privilege to assembly and to free speech is as applicable to those connected with the university as to all other citizens. . . . It will be the policy of the university to protect and to encourage these rights, limited only to their use under the rules applicable to all members of the university generally, and provided that such free speech and assembly is not inimical to the provisions and the spirit of the Constitution of the United States and the Constitution of the State of New Hampshire."[1]

College students are not children, but men and women, and should not be treated as children to whom certain discussions are forbidden. They are old

[1] *New York Times*, February 5, 1950.

enough to serve in our armed forces and, if need be, give their lives in defense of those things for which our nation stands, among which are freedom of speech and freedom of assembly. Many of them are voters; why should they not be encouraged to engage in political activities as a preparation for their much-needed participation after they leave college? These are things in which they are interested; they are proper interests, and the college should not interfere with them. Surely, political activity is as worthy as writing sports columns or concocting jokes for the college papers.

Moreover, candidates for office and other public figures should be allowed to speak before the campus political clubs. This will give students a chance to compare the rivals for office and evaluate the arguments for the policies of the respective parties. We talk of academic freedom, and properly so; surely the students have a right to similar freedom.

I should be glad to see a like opportunity opened to the various religious groups, be they Catholics, Protestants, Jews, Mohammedans, or Buddhists. It would be an excellent thing to allow them to hold meetings—not religious services—on the campus. One cannot at one and the same time preach the value of religion and deny it the opportunity to reach the students. But always the group should be a duly organized body with officers in charge, so that responsibility for anything untoward, should it arise, might be fixed.

In all the matters to which reference has just been made I have had in mind campus discussions in which students and professors participate, and which are open only to members of the university body. In short, a meeting should not be a device for gathering an audience of townspeople and spreading propaganda for this or that movement. The meetings should be intended for the intellectual stimulation of the student body, not as a sounding board for a "cause."

Much more difficult is the problem of inviting speakers from outside. Several factors must be borne in mind. In the first place, each speaker, once admitted, will thereafter be able to use, as a strong lever to gain speaking engagements at many other institutions, the argument that he was invited to speak on the campus of this or that university. More important than this, however, is the fact that the institution was built and supported by the state or by private benefactors not to serve as the Hyde Park of any and sundry agitators, but for the education of the young men and women who have the ability to justify that education. A college is not a circus ground for the presentation of this or that celebrity. Its buildings and equipment were designed to educate and train, not to serve as a platform for each and every crackbrained supporter of a myriad of causes. Should the university invite the proponent of "Ham-and-Eggs" or "Thirty Dollars Every Thursday" to speak before large assemblages? Its own respect for sound thinking would make it shrink from any such suggestion.

There are, of course, many speakers in a great variety of fields—government, the armed forces, education, religion, manufacturing, business—whom it would be a help to education for students to hear: a Charles Evans Hughes, an Elihu Root, a Stimson, a Marshall, a Hull, a Conant—examples such as these come readily to mind. On the other hand, there is on nearly every campus a small group of students, small, but vigorous and articulate, whose one and only desire is to bring upon the campus extreme leftists, partly in the hope that their clever propaganda may win adherents in the student body, partly to embarrass the administration of the college.

Personally, I think that from fear of public opinion, or of what is assumed to be public opinion, colleges tend to lean too far to the right in their attitude toward this question of inviting speakers. Provided only a proper balance is maintained, I see no reason in the world why liberals, so called, should not address the student body. Of course, I should resolutely bar out any extremist whose aim is clearly the overthrow of our form of government. The public has now been conditioned to treat Socialists as Communists and to eye askance anyone who has even a tinge of liberalism. But we must remember that by barring speakers with liberal views one does not keep young men and women from being liberal.

The solution is the creation of a faculty-student committee which shall have assigned to it the right of selecting the outside speakers, both liberals and conservatives, who are to be heard on the campus. It is important that the committee should include student representatives, for through them the faculty can find out what subjects and speakers the student body is genuinely interested in. I should bar those who are avowedly Communists or thoroughly established as such; I should also bar those who are known to be members of the Ku Klux Klan or of similar organizations that stir up hatred against men and women of other creeds or colors. Save for speakers of these types, I should not exclude any on the score of radicalism or reactionism. There should be no disinclination to invite labor leaders; quite the contrary, provided that a proper balance is maintained. So, too, for political and religious leaders. There is, as I have said, the danger that the faculty members may lean too heavily toward the side of caution; accordingly, those that are selected for this service should include a number who are distinctly liberal in outlook.

An address by a man or woman of distinction makes a significant contribution to the life of an institution. Because college curricula are numerous and varied, students have comparatively few common intellectual interests. An address by an eminent person gives them a common interest and provides material for many a discussion. Students, I know from my own experience, are anxious to hear representative men, and are stimulated in their thinking when the speakers really have something to say on almost any subject. I have seen a large auditorium filled with students to hear John Dewey—though I must admit that the audience to hear Knute Rockne was at least equally large.

I grant that sometimes a "committee on un-American activities" might be aroused because a particular speaker appeared on a college campus. The college should then stand on its rights and uphold the freedom of speech to which colleges have as much claim as any other group of Americans.

A debate between well-matched representatives of opposing views will be sure to command great interest and will bring out clearly the strength and weakness of the contending positions. In this way the legitimate desire of students to hear distinguished figures in our national life can be met, and in a fair manner.

XXIII.
Religion in the Colleges

ITS RELATION TO HIGHER EDUCATION

Great men are they who see that spiritual is stronger than any material force.

EMERSON

IT SEEMS strange to discuss the place of religion in American colleges when we remember that the earliest of them were founded for the training of clergymen. Nonetheless, it is a real question today in many institutions.

Obviously, for those which are avowedly under Catholic or Methodist or Quaker or other sectarian control there is no problem. Students who enroll in those colleges know what type of institutions they are and expect to attend chapel or mass, to have instruction in religious topics, and probably to find other courses slanted in accordance with views acceptable to the creed represented. But what should be the role of religion in private institutions which never had ties with any particular creed, or which, if they once had them, have severed their historical connection with a specific faith?

If its authorities believe that religion is an important, nay, an essential part of life, they will have a chapel on the campus. Very wisely, attendance at chapel is usually not made compulsory. And since the institution is not under the aegis of any special faith,

202

sermons should be delivered in turn by clergymen of different faiths, Catholic, Protestant, and Jewish; nor should I object to the presence of a Hindu or a Confucian priest. Since students may represent all forms of religious belief, they should not be limited to hearing sermons representing any one set of tenets in particular.

In view of the importance of religion, courses on its history, as well as on its philosophy, should be available to students. The instructor should be a profound scholar in his field; yet, without seeking to obscure the truth as he sees it, he should endeavor not to offend the sensibilities of the adherents of any faith.

When it comes to courses that may be called doctrinal, there is a difficulty. If they are given for any one faith, they should be offered for all. To ask a variety of clergymen to give the courses would be to descend from scholarship and the search for the truth to what would be undisguisedly propaganda. After all, the Catholic can and should go to his own church, where the appropriate instruction can be more fully and properly given and in an atmosphere suited to it. The same should be true of the Presbyterian student and the Christian Scientist. Assuredly, the discussion of religion save from a historical and philosophical point of view is not in harmony with the proper function of a college or university which is unaffiliated with a special creed. On the other hand, great encouragement should be given to student religious activities and to interfaith movements. Joint Thanksgiving Day services are admirable. And on all possible occasions college authorities should stress the import of religion in human life.

At the present day, and especially in our own country, we tend to forget the old religious wars and persecutions. History is stained with the blood of their victims; and the existence of a state religion was usually at the bottom of the trouble. Those who founded our government abhorred any possible connection between church and state and emphasized the right of every man to freedom of worship, and throughout the years every effort has been made to keep church and state apart. There has always been the fear that once the camel should push his head beneath the tent, he would soon thrust his whole body into it. It has been feared also that the religious differences existing in the general population, and in colleges between students, would be emphasized, and cleavages caused thereby. It has therefore seemed wisest to draw a sharp line between religion and all other public activities, in order that no one faith may dominate and that no religious test may be set up for any public function. And yet we do not hesitate to invite clergymen to offer prayer in the houses of Congress, or on academic occasions, even in public colleges. The nation and the several states in their interdict of religion in state institutions certainly cannot mean to subordinate religion or demean it; the utterances of our great public men constantly indicate religious belief, even as the words of Lincoln, "This nation under God shall have a new birth of freedom."

To be sure, round about many college campuses there are buildings devoted to student activities for the particular denominations or faiths which they represent, and these houses, Newman Hall, Hillel Foundation, Wesleyan Foundation, and the like, are centers for the students of these faiths, and there they associate with fellow students of their own creed for social purposes and for addresses. This is as far as many state universities have gone, but it should be noted that the university is concerned neither with their foundation nor their continuance. The public university does not, save in vague generalities, encourage attention to religion on the part of its students.

The problem of the state university is, of course, different from that of the private institution, and yet what I have proposed for the private, nonsectarian college ought not be impossible in a state university. Indeed, the latter should in every way repudiate the charge that it is godless by encouraging its students to attend the churches of their choice. Where there are no legal obstacles, I personally favor a chapel on the grounds of these institutions, to be used in turn under the auspices of the various faiths but not for religious observances. This does not in the slightest degree subject the institution to religious control, nor does it unite church and state. And assuredly the founders of our Constitution in calling for freedom of worship never intended to set up a ban against worship.

Jefferson himself made this clear: "It was not, however, to be understood that instruction in religious opinions and duties was meant to be precluded by the public authorities, as indifferent to the interests of society. On the contrary, the relations which exist between man and his Maker, and the duties resulting from those relations, are the most interesting and important to every human being, and the most incumbent on his study and investigation. The want of instruction in the various creeds of religious faith existing among our citizens presents, therefore, a chasm in a general institution of the useful sciences."[1] Presumably it was in harmony with Jefferson's views that the following regulation of the University of Virginia was adopted, on October 4, 1824: "Should the religious sects of this State, or any of them, according to the invitation held out to them establish within, or adjacent to, the precincts of the University, schools for instruction in the religion of their sect, the students of the University will be free, and expected to attend religious worship at the establishment of their respective sects, in the morning, and in time to meet their school in the University at its stated hour."[2]

The failure, too, of a university to give any attention to religion may well cause students to feel that religion is not only unimportant but unworthy of them. Physical education is treated as proper and necessary, but if the college is afraid of the very word "religion" it will cause its students, at the very time of their lives when questioning in all fields is uppermost, to regard religion as outside the roster of subjects worth considering. It will play a mighty part in sundering them from the church of their parents.

I should like to see the experiment made of offering, on the college campus, a series of lectures—not regular courses—affording to representatives of the several faiths an opportunity to present their points of

---

[1] *The Writings of Thomas Jefferson*, Definitive Edition, Andrew A. Lipscomb, editor-in-chief (Washington, D.C.: The Thomas Jefferson Memorial Association of the United States), Vol. XIX (1905), p. 414.

[2] See Roy J. Honeywell, *The Educational Work of Thomas Jefferson* (Harvard University Press, 1931), App. M, pp. 274–275.

view and their creed to a larger audience. For example, non-Catholics would thus be informed of the significance of the ritual of the Catholic Church, and as a result much prejudice might be broken down. These lectures would be attended voluntarily. They would have the advantage of revealing to students the nature of the different faiths; this knowledge is a part of the world of knowledge that should at least be accessible to all who are really seekers for the truth.

Not being a lawyer, I am unable to determine in what respect these proposals are legally permissible. In the case of McCollum vs. Board of Education, the Supreme Court ruled against "the use of tax-supported property for religious instruction"[3] and quoted from Everson vs. Board of Education: "Neither a state nor the Federal Government can set up a church. Neither can pass laws which aid one religion, aid all religions, or prefer one religion over another. . . . No tax in any amount, large or small, can be levied to support any religious activities or institutions, whatever they may be called, or whatever form they may adopt to teach or practice religion."[4]

There are, however, institutions such as the State University of Iowa, which even has a School of Religion in which instruction is given by a priest, a minister, and a rabbi, and the courses are duly accepted toward degree credit. These professors are supported in full by their particular groups and by contributions from individuals. The School is an integral part of the institution and "is based upon the following assumptions.

[3] No. 90, October Term, 1947.
[4] 330 U.S. 1.

"1. Religion is fundamental in any vital program of character education and hence should be given a place in the curriculum of any school.

"2. The responsibility for the development of religious education in a tax-supported institution should be shared by church and state."[5]

If the procedures at the University of Iowa are in accord with the Constitution as interpreted by the Supreme Court, then assuredly the modest proposals I have made are also.

The University of Kansas also has a School of Religion which "though not an organic part of the University offers courses for which students may receive credit."

The best thing a university can do is to encourage students each to seek the church of his own choice, and to stress the values that inhere in religion. Yet at the same time every precaution must be taken against even the slightest effort to press upon students any particular form of religion, or even religion itself. Important as most of us feel religion to be, it is yet more important for men and women to have freedom to reject it completely if they choose.

[5] University of Iowa Catalogue, 1946.

XXIV.

HOW DO THEY REGARD ALMA MATER?

There was an old woman who lived in a shoe.

MOTHER GOOSE

ALUMNI are of all kinds and types, even as children of any other mother. Some attain high distinction and bring glory to their Alma Mater. Others end in prisons, and the college is tempted to expunge their names from the Alumni Register. Many are "lost," so to speak; their whereabouts is unknown, and as far as the college is concerned they have disappeared completely. But there are others, and they are legion, who live good, uneventful lives, and who retain an interest in their college. Some evince an interest primarily in the institution as an educational center. By far the greater number express their concern with the college in enthusiasm for its athletic activities, particularly its football games.

At these games, very many of the spectators are alumni; and perhaps these are the only occasions on which they pay a visit to the campus. In their eyes, the football coach is more important than any member or members of the faculty, even more important than the president; but woe betide the coach if the team suffers a series of defeats! It is victories that are wanted, and nothing else counts. And sometimes it is victories at any cost.

As a result, there have arisen the barely concealed ways by which college athletics is professionalized and degraded. Clubs of alumni are formed ostensibly to back the team, but really to send backs (quarter, half, and full) to the college and naturally to the team. Each club member makes a contribution (it might be called "The 'V' for Victory Club"). On the other hand, rarely indeed does one hear that an alumnus has given financial aid to a brilliant student who will perhaps reflect glory on the college and whose contributions may even be significant to society.

When alumni honestly wish to give help to young men and women of promise, it should always be done through the established collegiate channels. In other words, no financial support in the form of a scholarship should be given except to those who are entitled to it in strict accordance with regular collegiate rules. This should bar out the athlete who is barely able to gain admission but who is far, very far, from eligibility to a scholarship bestowed by the college. It is admirable when alumni committees in various localities raise funds to be awarded as scholarships to promising boys and girls in their city or county who fully meet the college's requirements for such awards; but again, the application of the funds should be made through established collegiate channels.

Aside, however, from those who give monetary aid to athletes in one form or another, the alumni as a whole are carried away with ardent enthusiasm over sports, especially football. And colleges all too often lend themselves to this very state of affairs. They arrange alumni homecomings at the very time of important athletic contests, class reunions are scheduled to synchronize with these events, student-body gatherings are assembled and addressed by athletic coaches, athletes, or athletic alumni. The pages of alumni journals illustrate this predominant interest.

Alumni clubs exist in numerous cities and larger areas. Alumni living in a particular county or large city form an organization which meets at irregular times, sometimes to hear athletic addresses, sometimes to hear the president or other administrative officer of the college—though all too often, in the latter case, it is deemed good policy to attract a crowd by having an athletic representative also participate.

There are colleges which set up alumni visiting committees to give attention to the work and curricula of particular parts of the institution, for example, in engineering, medicine, law, and business administration. This practice is advantageous in stimulating among alumni a degree of concern with the educational purposes of the institution. The reports they submit naturally vary in value, but on the whole it is useful for a faculty to get the point of view of a selected group of alumni engaged in the profession for which training is being given. However, the faculty should not be too thin-skinned, for the visiting alumni are likely to see defects and weaknesses and frankly point them out.

Alumni journals should be useful means of "keeping alumni in touch" and informing them of changes and new developments in the college. Sometimes these journals fail to meet their obligations. A great scholar on the faculty may die and his career receive but a few lines of attention, while the athletic section of the publication is filled with details of the various games and players. It is, moreover, the college and its work which should be in the forefront, not the ideas of this or that alumnus on matters wholly unrelated to the college; for those views he can readily secure publicity in other journals.

Alumni organizations can and should be of the greatest value to the institution. The larger they are, the more potentiality for good exists. But it is the activity of the organization and its members that counts, not mere size. And while all such gatherings should possess the warm friendliness befitting children of a single mother, they need not descend to the undignified or the cheap. They should remember that they are children "of no mean mother." Through the journals, too, alumni should be kept in constant and intimate touch with the various aspects of the work of the college. Thus they can act as informed emissaries of the institution and help those in their communities who display an interest in it.

It is not unfair to expect them as recipients of the bounty of the college to be a means of securing financial support for it. If they are graduates of a state institution, they can and should be towers of strength with the local state senator and assemblyman; they can help citizens in their community who have not been college-trained to understand the value and importance of adequate support for the institution. It is their function to be unofficial lobbyists for their Alma Mater. They must remember, also, that they have received from the state an education costing thousands of dollars, more than they have paid in minor fees, and that the state has spent on them far more than on the vast majority of its citizens who have not been to college. Accordingly, when they have succeeded in their business or profession, it would be but proper that they make a fitting financial return. And similarly, graduates of independent colleges should gladly contribute to these institutions to the very limit their resources will permit, and should strive to interest persons of means in making contributions. In these days of rising costs and necessarily rising salaries (but with steadily decreasing returns from investments), private institutions will be in a desperate state unless alumni and friends help them bridge the great abyss in income.

In order to do this the more intelligently, the alumni should make the work of the college their primary interest, rather than feel concern whether the college team has defeated its hated rival in the annual football "classic." If alumni really regard the college as their Alma Mater, they should think of the nurture she gave them and seek to make a commensurate return. They should not only take this attitude, but in submitting suggestions to the college they should make them with humility, recognizing that their perspective on the work of the college as a whole is but a small one. On the other hand, the college authorities should remember that suggestions from alumni are made with real affection for the institution and reflect a valuable outside view of campus affairs.

The alumni should take advantage of the opportunities offered them to continue their education. Adult education is made available by many colleges; the study of the world's great literature and art adds to the richness of their lives, while at the same time they become better citizens of a democracy through fuller knowledge of national and international problems. Moreover, they will be interested in the college as an educational (not an athletic) institution and be of the greatest support in forwarding the purposes for which it exists.

XXV.

Honorary Degrees

BY VIRTUE OF THE AUTHORITY...

If it be a sin to covet honour.

King Henry V

MANY universities and colleges award honorary degrees. At each commencement, and often on other occasions such as a Founders' Day, candidates for the honor are formally presented to the president of the college, on a public platform, to hear him set forth in carefully phrased words the contributions each has made to mankind and then say, "By virtue of the authority vested in me by the trustees of this college, I confer on you the degree of Doctor of Laws." The hood symbolizing the doctorate, lined with the colors of the college, is slipped over the candidate's head, to hang upon his shoulders. And from that day forth he is entitled to be called "Doctor," though as an actual fact few make use of this privilege save those who are engaged in academic work and do not possess the degree of Doctor of Philosophy, and such clergymen as likewise have not received a doctorate in course. The latter are particularly eager to obtain the title, so that they may be on an equal plane with those of their colleagues who already have it.

In many institutions there is a faculty committee on honorary degrees which the president is required to consult before he makes his recommendations to the trustees. These committees, whose membership is secret, seek to be fair in their recommendations, I am sure. Since they seldom contain more than one member from any one department (say Music, or History), his influence, when there is consideration of a name in his field, is bound to be great. Of course, all members of the committee are likely to have opinions about well-known public figures. Names to be passed upon are submitted from various quarters, not infrequently in behalf of persons who have the slightest of claims to the proposed honor. The committees send in with their approval a very large number of names, and from among these the president makes his choice. Colleges for women naturally and properly consider that they are under a special obligation to give honorary recognition to women. Similarly, state institutions feel an obligation to honor citizens of the state or persons having some special connection with its affairs. Of course, neither type of institution limits its awards in this way.

Some colleges use such degrees as Doctor of Letters (Litt.D.) or Doctor of Humane Letters (L.H.D.) or Doctor of Science (Sc.D.) or Doctor of Music (Music D.). Some also grant decorations of the second class, so to speak, by giving honorary master's degrees. It is assuredly awkward when the recipient is conscious that, although he is regarded as worthy of honor, it is in a diluted form.

Unquestionably, the degree Doctor of Laws (LL.D.) is by far the most usual one for honorary purposes. Since it is not conferred in the United States to mark the completion of an academic program, it is clearly stamped as honorary. Some of the others, such as

Doctor of Science, are given by certain institutions in recognition of academic achievement; it is unfortunate, therefore, that this degree should be used also for honorary purposes, since a confusion necessarily results. When honorary master's degrees are conferred, as well as "regular" ones, confusion inevitably exists. It is certainly simplest to have but a single honorary degree; the necessity is thus obviated that the degree must indicate the field of the recipient's activity—a procedure which would result in a plethora of degrees, Doctor of Military Science, Doctor of Business Administration, Doctor of Public Affairs, and so on, conferred as honors. After all, the doctorate of laws has in reality no relation to law; the LL.D. is merely the doctor's degree *honoris causa*.

The question may be asked, "Why honorary degrees?" The answer is that in the United States no decorations are granted by the government in recognition of distinguished achievement, save in time of war. The universities, following the practice of European institutions, have stepped into the breach. It is but natural to wish to grant some token of appreciation to those who have done outstanding work in any field of human activity, and most human beings (however great) gladly receive the recognition.

Some institutions inflate the currency of their honorary degrees, as it were, by giving a host of them, so many indeed that they almost cease to be regarded as marks of distinction. Other colleges wisely limit the number to three or four at each academic ceremonial. This means, of course, a more rigorous sifting of names proposed; and the awards are then more likely to be bestowed on persons of real distinction or accomplishment. I have been struck, however, by the fact that the proportion of scholars, of members of college faculties, receiving honorary degrees is comparatively small. Among them I am not including college presidents or other administrative officers; presidents distribute these honors among themselves even as kings have always bestowed decorations on their fellow kings. One of our distinguished university presidents, a scholar in his own right, did not receive a single honorary degree while he was merely a professor, though eminent in his field; but since he assumed the presidential robes he has acquired a collection of thirty honorary titles.

Colleges and universities could easily determine who are the most eminent living historians, classical scholars, biologists, and bestow on them the accolade of the honorary degree. To be sure, if the graduate of a particular college later attains fame as a historian, his Alma Mater is pretty sure so to honor him. The tendency is, however, to seek "big names," whether of men in public life, in military affairs, in journalism, or in any other field of human activity. Is it not fair to assume that in part the college is seeking to "glamorize" its academic occasion by the presence of such eminent men and the conferring upon them of an honorary degree?

At times, it is hinted that degrees are conferred on persons of wealth in the hope of favors still to come. This is surely worshiping the golden calf and placing a doctor's hood on its shoulders. Sometimes the college may get its *quid pro quo,* but often the recipient feels no sense of obligation; he regards the honor as his due for his position in the world of finance. And if

218

he makes no return, it serves the college right for having sold its birthright for a mess of pottage. It is fair to say that the great universities are not often guilty of so questionable an act. Colleges may honor alumni who have won distinction; this is fitting and proper, for the mother who has sent forth her children very naturally takes pride in the achievements of her sons and daughters in the great outside world, and the alumni undoubtedly prize the recognition more than any other award which could possibly come to them.

An exemplary event at the Harvard Tercentenary celebration was the awarding of sixty-two honorary degrees, all to eminent scholars, indeed to scholars from all parts of the world. This precedent might well be followed by other institutions, especially on occasions of academic anniversaries.

Collection of honorary degrees automatically attaches to certain posts. I have already mentioned university presidents. Nicholas Murray Butler, of Columbia, probably "won the championship." In the last *Who's Who in America* published within his lifetime he listed 16 obtained in the United States and 21 in foreign lands, a total of 37. If Presidents of the United States wished to take time to pick up all that are offered to them, they could accumulate a sizable list. Herbert Hoover has a total of 50; it is fair to say that his work in European relief gave him an even larger number than he would have had as President alone. Cabinet officers, Supreme Court justices, high officers in the Army and Navy, are fair prey. Authors (especially poets) figure far less often; so, too, musicians and artists. Of course, any person, however prominent, suspected of ultraliberal views is likely to be passed by. Thus, Judge Brandeis did not receive a single honorary doctorate. Labor leaders are infrequently honored. It is indeed an interesting task to go over the list of recipients of honorary degrees; it gives a hint of the kind of achievement the American universities deem especially worthy of honor. One wonders how many such degrees Abraham Lincoln would have received, had he lived in these days when honorary degrees are bestowed by colleges at every crossroad.

XXVI.
The Forces That Shape the College

HIGHER EDUCATION DOES NOT
LIVE IN A VACUUM

Where there is no vision, the people perish.

Proverbs 29: 18

WE HAVE spoken of the part played in our colleges by trustees, president, deans, faculty, but behind them all the ultimate control rests definitely with the public. Of course, educational experiments may be planned and carried out by bold educational pioneers, but if they do not commend themselves to the public they will ultimately die.

Let us consider the two main types of colleges, public-supported and private or independent. However free of political influence the management of a state university may be, nonetheless in two ways the public can directly affect its work. One is through the grant of appropriations; the other is through the appointment by the governor of regents or trustees. Thus, if a state university should fail to support agriculture as fully as other activities—indeed should not do more for it than for work in other fields—the institution would very soon hear from the legislature, and in no uncertain voice. And legislatures have indirect

221

as well as direct ways of accomplishing their ends. They may of their own accord earmark large funds for purposes that interest them or their constituents; or they may threaten to cut other appropriations of the institution unless their pet projects are adequately cared for.

Aside from these direct means there are the indirect ones. Attacks from a considerable number of newspapers will have their effect on the institution. Letters from the local constituents of state legislators, especially petitions with many signatures, and, above all, resolutions which state formally the desires of organizations, not merely the powerful, but even those with a smaller number of members—all these command the attention of university administrative officers, and again and again are, in some measure at least, complied with. Sometimes the excuse may be given for their compliant action that it is better to yield here or there to the blast and thus protect the really significant and indispensable parts of the institution.

The most obvious pressures upon private colleges are those which are exerted by benefactors and alumni, who not infrequently are the same persons. These are not loath to tell the college what they think is right or wrong about the institution. And benefactors may have overwhelming and even unforeseen influence upon the work of a college; thus the bequest of the Wyman fortune to Princeton for a separate Graduate College resulted not only in the establishment of the College but also in the withdrawal of Princeton's then president, Woodrow Wilson.

Another public influence affecting these institutions is the movement of students to or from its gates. If a college does not meet the views of students and their parents, the students may well go elsewhere; and this vote by attendance or nonattendance will inevitably have its effect, for the tuition fees of students are essential if the running expenses of the college are to be met.

But I have been speaking only of the more or less obvious ways in which popular opinion affects the college. Behind it all is, of course, the general attitude of the public toward the institution. That extracurricular honors rate more highly than academic ones is due to the fact that society in our land deems presidencies of student bodies and editorships of student journals as really more important—more indicative of the qualities that make for success in life—than membership in Phi Beta Kappa. The judgment is a natural one, for in the world outside of college walls scholarship is not really esteemed. The extrovert who leads yells is far more likely to be chosen when a job is vacant than the "dig." In other words, our society sets up its own standards, and then esteems in college life the activities that conform to these. President W. H. P. Faunce of Brown University expressed this clearly and accurately: "I am inclined to think most Americans do value education as a business asset, but not as the entrance into the joy of intellectual experience or acquaintance with the best that has been said and done in the past. They value it not as an experience, but as a tool."[1] And Raymond D. Fosdick, head of the Rockefeller Foundation, has put it this way: "We have too easily made the assumption that other values would automatically follow our material well-being, that out

---

[1] Quoted by Abraham Flexner, *Universities, American, English, German* (Oxford University Press, 1930), p. 131.

of our assembly lines and gadgets the good life would spontaneously be born."[2] When the American people regard a leading historian as more important than the president of an automobile company, then will undergraduate scholarship be esteemed more highly than the "activities" of the "big shots" on the campus.

Again I would draw attention to the emphasis placed upon athletics. Students, being young and spirited, are naturally carried away by enthusiasm at athletic games; nonetheless, I think their ardors are fanned artificially by the sports pages of newspapers, which have so much to say about the successes or failures of college athletes. And to this add the attitude of a general public obsessed by athletics, a public to which the national championship baseball games are far more important than international happenings. Thousands pay exorbitant sums for tickets to the more popular college games and place large bets on the scores. I have noted that when college teams lose a series of games, the campus public is far less excited or downcast than the alumni, the press, and the general public. In short, I believe that much of the collegiate excitement over athletics is due to the attitude of these three elements in our society.

In a larger sense, the students' view of higher education is that of their parents, and, indeed, of the public as a whole: College is the normal place to go after leaving high school; college should help one make contacts valuable in later life; college through extracurricular activities gives training in "leadership"; college is a place where excessive work on academic subjects is deprecated; college offers fraternities and

[2] Report of the Foundation for 1947, p. 8.

sororities as good places to meet "the right people" and be decorated with insignia that will be useful in later years; college makes one eligible to the right clubs when college days are over; college will teach you how to make a living; college is a place for youthful enthusiasm and spirit; college is a place to which to return when you are middle-aged and prosperous and tell the students how you loafed when you were there and how the loafing made you what you are now. In short, in certain respects the American public's notions about college and university, and what they are for, have been a most potent force in making undergraduate college life what it is today. If the college is to be what it should be in making the American people really intelligent, well informed, and of good judgment, there is need of a great change of attitude on the part of parents and of the public as well. The press in publicizing what goes on at college reflects the interests of the public as a whole.

I do not for a moment mean to imply that there is no intellectual interest among students; there unquestionably is a considerable number of students who gain much from the scholarly work of the college or university. But I am speaking of the general atmosphere of the institutions, not of the attitude of the exceptional student. Among those who do obtain scholastic honors there are, indeed, some who have scattered their energies among their studies and extracurricular activities; but though they have been able, in spite of scattered effort, to attain high rank in their classes, they have failed by far to make the most of the opportunities the college offers.

The vulgarization of campus life is not surprising when one views it in the light of certain aspects of American life as a whole. Fashion shows in campus buildings, the selection of "queens" for this or that organization or class, sometimes termed by the elegant scholarly word "dolls," female colonels of cadets, pictures of so-called campus leaders (male and female) parading as models for the offerings of clothing stores, female newspaper hawkers screaming their wares on the public streets, majorettes, female yell leaders— this list could be extended to a great length. But in all this, college is merely aping the outside world. If there is a queen for fishmongers' day, why not for the sophomore class? Not only do these things vulgarize the campus; they also play their part in rendering scholarship less important—or even unimportant.

Is it surprising, then, that when college graduates go out into the world they are so often indistinguishable from their fellow citizens who did not share their advantages? Their language certainly is no different, no better. It almost appears as if they wished to assume a protective coloration so as not to be marked out from their fellows. Their reading matter is the same—the same popular (or rather, widely read) weeklies, the same magazines, the same "funny" pages, the same sporting green. In the barber shop, college graduates are as much interested as the bootblacks in discussing the sports pages, the baseball games, the scores of the major baseball contests, the playing of the heroes of the diamond, and possess a store of historical lore on the championship series.

It has become, in short, a vicious, a deadly circle; the public sends its sons and daughters to college with certain nonacademic goals in mind; they come forth but little influenced by the scholarly side of the college; they sink into the plane of the community from which they came. Under such circumstances how can our colleges supply adequate intellectual leadership to society and to the nation? Desperately do we need it, but the public's fundamental scorn of the processes of the mind defeats the aims of the college.

To be sure, college sends men out who become presidents of this or that local club or board—yes, state legislators and officials, and even national legislators. But, in any real sense, how many of these are leaders? They know the tricks of presiding, the way to pat others on the back and be a good fellow, the devices to win votes, the wisecracks that are applauded; but how much do they really contribute to the life of the community?

And from this accordingly arises the fact that, with certain obvious exceptions, our leaders in the various branches of government—national, state, and city—are so often mediocre. The radio reveals this with deadly clarity to those who listen to the forums, debates, or speeches. Not to speak of the English which all too often they murder, they display no flashes of intellectual power, no keenness of mind, and likewise often no courage when they deal, as sometimes they must, with controversial subjects.

Consider for a moment the quality of the men in the convention which framed our federal Constitution. Remember that they were drawn from a tiny stretch of territory containing a population of somewhat less than four millions. Then read their speeches, read such writings as appear in *The Federalist*, and compare

227

them with the *Congressional Record* of today. Why
should there be so glaring a contrast? I believe it is
because the people of the earlier time selected their
representatives on the basis of character and intelligence, and did not have "representatives" foisted upon
them by the tricks of politicians. The public of that
day did not glorify the "go-getter"; it esteemed intellectual leaders and the things of the mind. Franklin
said of the delegates, "We have here at present what
the French call *une assemblée des notables,* a convention composed of some of the principal people from
the several states of our Confederation."[3] And casting
this esteem upon the waters, they received a manifold
return. The colleges of the day, young as they were,
and weak, according to the lights of their day stressed
learning, for such was the desire of the society they
served.

Read your Jefferson, your Franklin, and you will see
how the things of the mind came first; and yet both
men mentally ranged over fields that extended far and
wide. They and their associates were genuinely intellectual; whether they went to college or not was of no
moment.

How, then, shall this vicious circle be broken? It is
not easy to set out to mold or bend public opinion.
The colleges must seek to break the circle by fighting
tooth and nail against the deification of "success boys";
they must not yield to the glorification of the trade
school in their curricula. It will not be an easy fight,
but in a generation the success of the new orientation
should begin to manifest itself.

[3] Carl Van Doren, *The Great Rehearsal* (New York: Viking Press,
1948), p. 13.

If a stand is not made soon, the college as a center of learning, save in the training of specialists and the researches of its faculty, will shed a very feeble light. The excrescences of college life must be relentlessly removed. The time wasted on the gossip of the campus in the college newspaper had far better be spent on history or economics; the young man aiming at a political career had better learn what the past has to teach him than to spend his time devising ways to gain votes for the student-body presidency. If you point out to me that many of those graduates whose careers are termed successful were "Big Men" on the campus, I should have two replies: (1) When they were undergraduates, student activities did not by any means consume as large a part of a student's time as they do at present—an increase of distraction that is due not only to the growth of student bodies, but also to the increase in emphasis on student prominence. (2) When such a type of prominence is given priority in the minds of students, efforts to gain such honors will inevitably divert from absorption in scholarly pursuits those who have the potentialities of great scholarly attainments. These men would have been able to play their part no less effectively in the world if they had not been so conspicuous in the extracurricular life of the campus; indeed, had they directed that time to academic pursuits, they would have come to public careers with a far richer background.

Not only must the college strive to make itself more nearly what it was designed to be, but its graduates must have reflected to them again and again from responsible sources what the true ideals of an educated man should be. Alumni gatherings which present on an equal footing athletic coaches and distinguished scholars play a significant part in giving graduates a distorted view of their relative importance. College graduates should be urged to live the lives of educated men, and not be ashamed of being educated; they should be stimulated not merely to hear an occasional address on some important subject, but to read the books that have intrinsic value. The kind of reading that educated men do should mark them out as educated men.

I grant that newspapers must cater to the popular craze for athletics. But I wish with all my heart that, in the future interest of the boys who compete, the press would lower the candlepower of the electric lights they play upon them and their activities; to make those boys appear as important as great public men is doing them a great disservice. And, on the other hand, cannot the newspapers give more attention to the scholarly activities of the college and emphasize too the scholarly achievements of the undergraduates? When Phi Beta Kappa elects to membership the distinguished scholars of each class, surely each one chosen deserves at least two or three lines of type on this one occasion, as compared with the columns given to a halfback or a pitcher. Surely, prizes and other academic honors should be worthy of being at least reported by the press.

And in the college itself activities should be played down. A student-body president is not necessarily one to be made as much of as the most brilliant student of the class. College newspapers must learn to change their emphasis, even though college editors may have no sympathy with paying attention to "digs." And college officials must cease talking out of two sides of their mouths, on solemn academic occasions lauding scholarly aims and high ideals, but at athletic rallies burning incense before the athletic gods. In short, the college can render its greatest service to society by returning to the ideals which brought it into being. I am not speaking of curricula or courses, but of that which is behind and above all curricula, the aim to minister to the intellectual development of students and thereby of society as a whole.

With all its weaknesses, democracy has revealed itself as the best form of government yet established for mankind. The problem we are facing is whether we cannot so restore our institutions of higher education to the principles which in their early days animated them, that they will raise the general level of intelligence and make our citizens still more able to bear the heavy burdens which democracy brings. Can they not aid in creating a respect for learning and for those who are truly educated? Can they not among the throng who resort to them train those who have the capacity and integrity, so that without regard to their origin they will be chosen as the best leaders for this democracy of ours? In our various legislative bodies, state and national, and in our various executive posts, we must help democracy by having ready for her service many men and women of broad knowledge, of ripe wisdom, and of the purest character. Then shall our colleges be performing one of their highest functions.

It cannot be denied that nowhere else in the world does so large a proportion of the population receive higher education; in no land is so much money being spent on education as a whole. We have here a foundation on which we should build an edifice worthy of our democracy. We admit, too, that our institutions have done admirable work in training professional men and women in a great variety of fields. We admit, too, that despite the criticism I have just directed at the atmosphere of our colleges there are those who have gained much intellectually from what the colleges have to offer. But when one thinks of the potentialities that reside in the education of hundreds of thousands of our young people in each generation, he longs for a change of attitude, an elevation of standards, that will mean much in the life of our people.